The Changing Nature of Warfare

By Alex Kerr

Edited by Kartik Thyagaraja & Liberal Publishing House

Bullet text: First Edition

Preface:

This book intends to give as much information as possible about the history of warfare and to relate it to the IGCSE Edexcel exam board.

Alex Kerr has been teaching History and Politics for ten years. He is a graduate of Oxford Brookes University and has completed a PGCE at The Institute of Education, London as well as recently completing courses at the Johann Cruyff Institute, Barcelona.

The book will cover:

- The nature of warfare in the early 1930s (This will include a brief introduction to weapons through WW1)
- Changing methods of land warfare
- Changing methods of sea and aerial warfare
- The development of atomic and nuclear weapons
- Warfare at the beginning of the 21st century

Answering Questions on the Changing Nature of Warfare:

Remember it is not just **Change** it is also **Continuity**.

- ✓ How does warfare change?
- ✓ How does warfare stay the same?

This is a breadth study, so key aspects need to be learnt.

1. The changing nature of warfare, 1919-39
2. Changing methods of warfare by land, sea and air, 1939-45
3. New forms of conflict – nuclear and guerrilla warfare versus conventional warfare, 1945-75
4. Conventional warfare and the development of 'new' wars, 1976-2000
5. Changing methods of warfare at the beginning of the 21st century, 2000-10

The themes can be broken down into 5 points:

These are:

1. Land warfare
2. Sea warfare
3. Air warfare
4. Weaponry, technology and communications
5. Guerrilla warfare
6. Future warfare

The exam paper is divided into three questions:

It is also divided into three question types:

(a): This focuses on in what ways things changed (or stayed the same). Students respond by offering two such ways.

(b): This focuses on causation. Students write an account that explains two causes of an event.

(c): There are two questions, and the student must choose one: either a question that shows the extent of change, or the significance of a factor in war.

Contents

Chapter 1; War, huh, what is it good for?

Chapter 2; The Nature of Warfare in the early 1930's.

Tanks, Navy, Military Aircraft, Artillery and Gas.

Chapter 3; The Changing Nature of Sea Warfare.

Battle of the Atlantic, Nuclear Submarines, Aircraft Carriers, Battle of the Pacific including, Pearl Harbour, Battle of the Coral Sea and the Battle for Midway and The Falklands Conflict.

Chapter 4; Land Warfare during WW2.

Blitzkrieg, Invasion of Poland, Invasion of the Low Countries and France, Operation Barbarossa and Battle of the Bulge.

Chapter 5; The Changing Nature of Air Warfare.

The Battle of Britain, The Blitz, V weapons and the Allied bombing of Germany.

Chapter 6; Middle Eastern Conflicts

The Six Day War, The War of Yom Kippur, the First Gulf War, and the Second Gulf War.

Chapter 7; Guerrilla Warfare

Purpose of Guerrilla Warfare or Blitzkrieg, Blitzkrieg vs Guerrilla Strategy, Strategy and Tactics of Guerrilla Warfare, Vietnam War and Afghanistan War.

Chapter 8; Amphibious Operations

World War 2: D-Day, what was the Allies' plan? And Deception: Operation Bodyguard.

Chapter 9; Airborne Operations

World War 2, Arnhem.

Chapter 10; The Atom Bomb

Reasons for dropping atom bombs in 1945 and the Bombing of Hiroshima

Chapter 11; Cold War

The Cold War, The Nuclear Arms Race, The Arms Race 1945-60, ICBMs, Mutual Assured Destruction (MAD Theory), The Arms Race 1960-91, MIRVs, Détente and Arms Reduction Talks, Attempts at Arms Limitation and End of the Arms Race.

Chapter 12; 21st Century

Warfare at the beginning of the 21st century, Impact of Terrorism, Different types of Terrorist Acts, 9/11, High-Tech Weapons, The Arms Race 1960-91, MIRVs, Détente and Arms Reduction Talks, Attempts at Arms Limitation and End of the Arms Race.

Glossary

Key terms:

Asymmetric warfare: A war between two or more opposing groups whose military power differs, or whose strategy or tactics differ significantly. For example, this could be and usually is a war between a professional army against an insurgency, guerrilla army or resistance movement.

Proliferation: the increase in numbers of nuclear or chemical weapons, or weapons in general.

Strategy: a plan of action designed to achieve a long-term or overall aim. (Large plan.)

Tactics: a military action that is carefully planned to achieve a specific goal, within the strategy. (Little plan.)

Glossary for Land Warfare WWI

Artillery: large guns firing shells

Bombardment: long and heavy firing at targets (also used at D-Day by navy ships)

'No Man's Land': land between the two lines of trenches

Barbed wire: wire with barbed spikes (placed in 'No Man's Land')

Trenches: ditches dug out of the ground for defence

Zeppelins: German airships (bombed London)

Reconnaissance: looking (observing & photographing) from planes in WWI

Glossary for Land Warfare WWII

Motorised transport: various vehicles run with gasoline used to move soldiers

Outflanked: forces come from the side to attack

Reinforcements: extra troops join the battle

'Maginot Line': line of concrete defences built by the French to protect themselves from German attacks

Panzer tanks: type of German tank, powerful and heavily armed.

'Scorched earth': destroying everything often by burning it, then leaving

'Atlantic Wall' lines of German defences along the northern French coast to defend against possible invasion from Britain/USA

Luftwaffe: German air force

RAF: British air force

Mulberries: floating harbours used in Normandy by Britain & USA

Whales: bridges for mulberries to land.

Amphibious: vehicles that can go on land and water, e.g. DUKW (Duck vehicle)

Bobbin: a tank that lays carpet road on the beach.

Pluto: Underwater oil pipe.

Significant Wars: Battle of the Atlantic, Battle of the Pacific, Battle of Britain, The Blitz, invasion of Poland, Western Europe, Soviet Union, D-Day, Arnhem and Battle of the Bulge.

Glossary for Land Warfare after 1945

Coalition: group of countries fighting together

Guerrilla: a type of warfare, including tactics such as hit and run. Small groups, rather than large armies, attack when the enemy is weak.

Mujahideen: Islamic guerrilla fighters in Afghanistan

Sabotage: destroying something, e.g. power lines, pipelines

Terrain: the land, e.g. mountains, jungle, forest etc

Morale: the enthusiasm of people

Booby traps: traps for soldiers (fall into a spiked pit etc.) often set-off by a wire

Search and destroy: Tactic used by the US in Vietnam. Helicopters bring in soldiers, they attack a specific area such as a village, then leave

Vietcong: a communist political organization in South Vietnam, who used Guerrilla tactics.

Significant battles: 6-day war, War of Yom Kippur, Vietnam War, Afghanistan, Falklands War, Cold-War, First Gulf War, Second Gulf War.

Terrorist Groups

Hijacking/Skyjacking: the taking of a vehicle or plane

Assassination: the killing of someone

War on Terror: US war against terrorism after 9/11

9/11: Terrorist attack on US, New York, 2001 by terrorist group Al-Qaeda.

Black September: Pro-Palestinian group, who fought against Israel by kidnapping 11 Israeli athletes.

Hamas: Pro-Palestinian group fights against Israel.

IRA/Irish Republican Army: Pro-Irish independence group who fought against Britain for full independence.

Hezbollah: Anti-Israel group, fought against the invasion of Lebanon.

Resistance movements: An organised effort by some of the civilian population of a country to fight against the established government or occupying power, with the aim of disrupting civil order and stability.

Significant events: 9/11.

Glossary for Sea Warfare after 1939

Blockade: stopping supplies getting into a city or country (e.g. the blockade of Germany in WWI)

U boats: German submarine

Submerge: go underwater (submarine)

Wolf Pack: groups of U boats attacking ships

Merchant ships: non-military vessels carrying cargo and supplies

Depth charges: explosives used to blow up submarines (rolled off the back of ships)

Hydrophones: an underwater listening device (to find U-boats)

Convoy: a group of something travelling together (ships)

Torpedo: missile shot by submarines

Q-boats: name for boats that look like merchant ships, but were armed

Enigma code: German code, broken by British (Alan Turing and the first computer)

ASDIC or sonar: transmitted sound waves out - if they hit an object(submarine) underwater, echo signals were sent back, so U boats could be found

Air gap: an area where British/US planes could not reach

Hunter killers: British warships that went after U boats

Hedgehogs: anti-submarine mortars fired from ships

Task force: a group of warships (mix of aircraft carriers, destroyers, supply ships etc.)

Aircraft carriers: ships from which planes could take off and land

Dive bombers: aircraft with large bombs, attacking a target by diving from high up.

Significant battles: Battle of the Atlantic, Battle of the Pacific, the Cold War, Falklands, First and Second Gulf War.

Glossary for Air Warfare after 1939

Blitz: (lightning) fast, violent attack

London Blitz: the bombing of the city by the Germans

Evacuees: people moved from an area of danger (especially children out of British cities during the bombing by the Germans)

Reinforcements: extra troops join the battle

Civilians: ordinary people, not fighting people (not army)

Chemical weapon: a munition (bomb) which causes injury/death through chemicals

Luftwaffe: German air force

Messerschmitt & Stuka dive bomber: German fighter planes

RAF: British air force

Hurricanes & Spitfires: British fighter planes

Air superiority: name for having control of the air over the enemy

Air cover: protection by air

Incendiary bombs: bombs made to cause fires (napalm)

V rockets: first long-range missiles (V1-V2 rockets)

Rolling Thunder: name is giving to the bombing of North Vietnam by US Stealth aircraft planes that avoid being seen by radars.

Glider: Plane with no engine, requires a plane with an engine to take off.

Significant Battles: Battle of Britain, Arnhem.

Glossary for nuclear & high-tech weapons

Atomic bomb or fission bomb: works by splitting the atom to cause an explosive chain reaction

Hydrogen bomb or thermonuclear bomb: works like a fission bomb but using more plutonium to create a more powerful explosion

Nuclear bomb: all bombs using a nuclear reaction - atomic or hydrogen - which use a small amount of matter to release huge amounts of energy

Manhattan Project: name was given to the project to develop the first atomic bomb

MAD/Mutual Assured Destruction:

ICBM: Intercontinental Ballistic Missile - missile than is fired from one continent and can reach another - uses rockets plus gravity to fall onto its target

IRBM: Intermediate Range Ballistic Missile - less range than ICBM but more accurate

Sputnik: name of first (USSR) satellite in space (transmitted a radio signal back to earth)

Cuban Missile Crisis: USSR attempted to place nuclear missiles on the island of Cuba, USA objected - a stand-off between the two until USSR agreed to remove missiles (risk of nuclear war between US & USSR)

Détente: reducing nuclear missiles.

Polaris Submarines: type of submarine that can fire nuclear missiles.

Non-proliferation: stop the spread of nuclear weapons.

Kidnapping: this is taking someone against their will.

Hostage: taking someone & demanding something for their return.

Drone: remote-controlled aircraft.

GPS/Global Positioning Satellite: using several satellites to fix a position.

Conventional weapons: non 'high tech' weapons, e.g. tanks, soldiers, artillery etc.

Laser guided weapons: weapons that use a laser to guide them to their target.

Cruise Missile: a guided missile.

Scud: a tactical ballistic missile developed by the Soviet Union, able to move around on a vehicle.

JDAM/Joint Direct Attack Munition: Laser guided bomb.

JSOW/Joint Standoff Weapon: Missile that can change direction.

HPM/High Powered Microwave: a bomb that releases an electrical charge.

Smart weapons: Weapons that can use an onboard computer to guide themselves to their targets.

Significant Events: Hiroshima and Nagasaki, the Cuban Missile Crisis, and Star Wars.

Timeline

1931 Japanese invasion of Manchuria

1935 Italian invasion of Abyssinia

1936 Beginning of the Spanish Civil War

1937 Bombing of Guernica

Bombing of Shanghai

1939 End of the Spanish Civil War

The beginning of World War Two

1940 Blitzkrieg used against the Low Countries and France

The Battle of Britain begins

The beginning of the Blitz on Britain

1941 Operation Barbarossa begins the German invasion of the Soviet Union

Japan attacks America at Pearl Harbor

1942 Battle of the Coral Sea

Battle of Midway

1943 Allied invasion of Italy

Battle of the Philippine Sea

1944 D Day

Operation Market Garden

Battle of Leyte Gulf

German use of V1 and V2 weapons

1945 US combined operations at Iwo Jima and Okinawa

Atom bombs dropped on Hiroshima and Nagasaki

End of World War Two

1949 Soviet Union tests its first atom bomb

1950 Beginning of the Korean War

1952 USA tests its first hydrogen bomb

1953 Soviet Union tests its first hydrogen bomb

1963 Partial Nuclear Test Ban Treaty

1965 First US combat troops in Vietnam

1967 Outer Space Treaty

1971 Sea-bed Treaty

1972 Strategic Arms Limitation Treaty (SALT 1)

Biological Warfare Convention

1973 US withdrawal from Vietnam

1975 Helsinki Agreements

1979 Soviet invasion of Afghanistan

Strategic Arms Limitation Treaty (SALT 2 – never ratified)

1982 Falklands War

1983 USA announces the Strategic Defence Initiative (SDI)

1987 Intermediate Nuclear Forces Treaty (INF)

1989 Soviet withdrawal from Afghanistan completed

1990 Iraq invades Kuwait. First Gulf War

Conventional Armed Forces in Europe Treaty (CFE)

1991 End of First Gulf War

The first use of Tomahawk cruise missiles

Strategic Arms Reduction Treaty

1992 Beginning of the war in Bosnia

1995 End of the war in Bosnia

2001 9/11 attacks in the USA

2003 Beginning of the Second Gulf War

2004 Madrid bombing

Beslan School hostage crisis

2005 London bombings

Helpful Hints for teachers and students:

You will need to learn about the fundamental concepts relevant to this study:

asymmetric warfare	Blitzkrieg	laser	proliferation	resistance movements	tactics
Blitz	drones	MAD theory	smart weapons	strategy	technology

Significance: This is the influence or meaning of an impact on an event or the change the event has had. It can also be regarded as the importance of that impact. E.g. *The significance of 9/11 was that the West had to take the threat of terror attacks more seriously and change the approach to dealing with Islamic fundamentalism.*

Impact: This is how powerful the effect that something, especially some new change, has on a situation or person. E.g. *The use of the atom bomb had a tremendous impact on the superpowers because of this the Soviet Union retaliated by developing its own atomic weapons, and as a result, the arms race started.*

Continuity and Change: This is one of the most important parts of the course and gaining the most marks. You need to talk about what stayed the same over a more extended period and what changed over that period of time, e.g. during D Day and Arnhem in 1944 the U.S. and U.K. used combined operations in war, as seen were still used as essential techniques as in the Falkland War (1982) and the Gulf War (1990-91). However, significant change did take place with the onset of asymmetric warfare seen in the Guerilla warfare of Vietnam during the 1960s.

Consequence: This means what happened because of an action, in other words, it is the result of an event or change. E.g. *A result of the development of the inter-continental ballistic missile (ICBM) was the acceleration in the build-up of nuclear weapons by the U.S.A and U.S.S.R, the two main superpowers of the era. Both superpowers were concerned by the other's ability to deliver atomic warheads and so raced to have as many ICBMs as possible.*

Chapter 1:

War, huh, what is it good for?

***

Let's get started:

United States Admiral Gene La Rocque served during World War 2:

"I hate it when they say. 'He gave his life for his country.' Nobody gives his life for his country.' Nobody gives their life for anything. We steal the lives of these kids. We take it away from them. They don't die for honour and glory of their country. We kill them."

Adolf Hitler, (Leader of Germany during 1933 - 1945) Mein Kampf, Chapter 11. "The struggle between the various species does not arise from a feeling of mutual antipathy but rather from hunger and love. In both cases, Nature looks on calmly and is even pleased with what happens. The struggle for the daily livelihood leaves behind in the ruck everything that is weak or diseased or wavering; while the **fight** of the male to possess the female gives to the strongest the right, or at least, the possibility to propagate its kind. And this struggle is a means of furthering the health and powers of resistance in the species. Thus it is one of the causes underlying the process of development towards a higher quality of being."

Although Hitler does not directly say this, a few actions do suggest that he was keen for war, to eradicate what he perceived to be inferior people to allow the strong to survive; a negative twist on Darwinian Theory. Warfare would be a way of ridding the Nazis of the weak, whilst allowing the strongest to survive.

Think about what these quotations and perspectives say about warfare, how they contrast and the points that both men are trying to convey.

Does war have any positive aspects to it?

Advances in medicine and technology, such as the atom bomb or nuclear power plants.

How significant are the effects of war?

There was significant political change, protest, loss of life, the profound effects on society and the questions of morality.

Why is this course relevant and significant to students and teachers?

Wars continue to this day.

This has led to terrorism, which is now a significant part of society.

The course can even show students and teachers that leaders of the Western World still do not understand the significance of their good and bad decisions in warfare.

Barack Obama and drone attacks.

Donald Trump and recent bombing raids in Afghanistan.

Chapter 2:

The Nature of Warfare in the early 1930's

***

This section will look at methods of warfare changing from World War 1, the interwar years to World War 2:

- Tanks
- Navy
- Military Aircraft
- Artillery
- Gas

World War 1 (July 1914 – November 1918)

A total war, with fighting centred on Europe, with further smaller scale conflicts taking place elsewhere in the world. One group of allies was the British Empire, the French Empire, and the Russian Empire, who fought against Germany, the Austria-Hungarian Empire and the Ottoman Empire. Many other countries were involved in this conflict.

The fighting was fierce and involved millions of men, whilst also bringing in the countries' home fronts, where children and women were brought into the war economy to help in any way they could.

On land, the main things to think about and remember are the weapons and style of warfare employed, which leads to significant changes taking place during World War I and afterwards.

- Trenches
- Tanks
- Gas
- Artillery
- Machine guns

You also need to remember that this is a move from a relatively stationary war, between infantry, (mobile through cavalry and trains) where men fought in trenches, and would move across 'no man's land' (an area of unoccupied land with trenches either side, held by two or more opposing sides) to a more mobile war, with the use of tanks, infantry, airpower, artillery and cavalry, all coordinating together.

Source:

Sir Douglas Haig, September 1916. *"Gueudecourt was carried after the protecting trench to the west had been captured in a somewhat interesting fashion. In the early morning, a Tank started down the portion of the trench held by the enemy from the north-west, firing its machine guns and followed by bombers (Men carrying Mills Bombs). The enemy could not escape, as we held the trench at the southern end. At the same time, an aeroplane flew down the length of the trench, also firing a machine gun at the enemy holding it. These then waved white handkerchiefs in token of surrender, and when this was reported by the aeroplane, the infantry accepted the surrender of the garrison. By 8.30 A.M. the whole trench had been cleared, great numbers of the enemy had been killed, and 8 officers and 362 other ranks made prisoners. Our total casualties amounted to five."*

Question for students to think about:

This is a significant event in warfare, can you see why?

Answer:

This is the first time that the warfare had become co-ordinated between land and air, as well as vehicles and infantry.

World War 2 (September 1939 – September 1945)

On 1 September 1939, the Germans began their World War II campaign with the invasion of Poland. Germany invaded Poland under false pretences. They claimed that the Poles had carried out a series of sabotage operations against Germany near the German/Polish border. Extra note: It is also important to bear in mind that the Soviet Union also invaded Poland as well as nearby countries.

On the 10th of May 1940, the Germans launched their attack on Western Europe, France, Belgium, Holland and Luxembourg. By June 12, 1940, the Germans had achieved victory over Belgium, Holland, Luxembourg, France and Britain, culminating in the mass evacuation at Dunkirk. Britain would not return to occupy Europe again until 6 June 1944.

Shocked by their experience, the Allied observers who survived the collapse of France viewed the defeat as an entirely new form of war pioneered by the German army (Wehrmacht). It had seemed as if German tanks and aircraft were everywhere. Blitzkrieg seemed to be based on the spread of new technology, Aircraft, Tanks, military vehicles, cavalry and followed by infantry.

Tanks

The development of tanks during the First World War was a response to the stalemate that trench warfare had created on the Western Front. During the war, both sides had discussed and attempted to design vehicles incorporating the basic principles of tanks (armour, firepower, and all-terrain mobility.) It was the heavy casualties sustained in the first few months of hostilities that stimulated development. The research took place in both Great Britain and France, with Germany following the Allies' lead.

The first tanks were mechanically unreliable. There were problems that caused considerable loss rates during combat and transit. The heavily shelled terrain was impassable to conventional vehicles, and only highly mobile tanks such as the Mark and FTs performed reasonably well. The Mark I's rhomboid shape, caterpillar tracks, and 26 feet length meant that it could navigate obstacles, especially wide trenches that wheeled vehicles could not.

After World War I, General Ludendorff of the German High Command praised the Allied tanks as being a key reason in Germany's defeat. The Germans had been too slow to recognise the value of tanks and develop them. Even if their industry could have produced them in large quantities, the Germans did not have the fuel to run them. The Germans fielded 90 tanks in total by the end of World War One, and 75 of those 90 had been captured by the Allies.

At the war's end, the central role of the tanks was close support of the infantry.

By 1929, many British students of armour preferred the idea of a pure armour formation; German General Heinz Guderian had become convinced that it was useless to develop just tanks, or even to mechanize parts of the traditional arms, such as trucks or support cars. General Guderian believed that an entirely new mechanized formation was needed that would maximize the effects of the tank.

Due to the tactics and strategy of the Germans in World War II, many armies were forced armies to integrate all the available weapons into a mobile, flexible unit. In 1939, most armies still thought of an armoured division as a mass of tanks with little support from other areas of the military. By 1943, this had all changed; the same armies had evolved. The armoured divisions were now a balance of different arms and services, each of which had to be as mobile and as protected as the tanks.

Due to this development, infantry units in Germany, the Soviet Union, and America developed tank support vehicles, such as tank destroyers and assault guns.

So, you would not just have tanks. Ideally, you would want tanks, armoured cars and trucks, cavalry, infantry and cover from the air and artillery if you were to be successful. This would then have to be supported by fuel, ammunition and food (known as supplies or logistics). Pretty complicated as you can imagine.

The effects of Tanks:

The tank was the most unique new weapon, which was to have long-lasting significance for land warfare. In World War 1, tanks provided a psychological boost for British troops, provided cover for forces, and were able to blast and bulldoze their way through enemy lines or at the very least drive over the top of them. However, they had a limited impact in the First World War. In 1918 they were used as a battering ram supported by the infantry. Moreover, by 1918 the Germans had developed armour-piercing machine-gunned bullets and had adapted field-guns to fire at tanks, which were large, slow and therefore easy targets.

The Spanish Civil War 1936 - 39:

The Spanish Civil War was one of the most significant wars in between the First and Second World Wars. It involved Spain as well as three major powers, the Soviet Union, Italy and Germany. In total, roughly 500,000 to 600,000 people were killed, and it had extensive media coverage. It started as a Spanish war and was soon co-opted by Fascists and Communists.

Background:

King Alfonso the Thirteenth launched a disastrous war against Morocco in the 1920s. By 1931 Alfonso the Thirteenth had left the country due to a weak economy and lacking support from the military. A new Republic government was created under Niceto Alcala-Zamora. Niceto promised liberal changes and modernisation and autonomy for the Basque Country and Barcelona. The changes were slow, and with a world economic depression, the left and right wings of politics felt more and more alienated. In 1934, communists and anarchists rose up in rebellion against the new Catholic party that had won recent elections and had gained power in central government. By 1936 a new left-wing government had been created, Niceto left, and Manuel Azana was elected to power, and officers in the military were changed or removed to stop a coup. However, this was not enough, and a coup was started under General Franco in Morocco, which caused generals to rise in every city and forced the police to join with the leftists. This caused the country to split between the Nationalists and the Republicans. The Government had control of Madrid, Barcelona and Valencia. Republicans were ruthless, with any dissenters, and Republican supporters wanted to destroy large amounts of material that would remind them of the old ways.

The Republicans were disunited in their aims; the Government wanted to hold on and survive. The Communists and Anarchists wanted to create a utopia.

Use of tanks and aircraft in the Spanish Civil War

Franco's strategy was simple; it would involve using sheer numbers of troops to conquer Spain. Madrid's resistance altered that program. Franco sought to eliminate all the partisans (Communists and Anarchists) of the Republic by driving through all of Spain, starting in the south, and driving along the northeast of Spain. The Republics strategy was basically to hinder that. It was a defensive plan with no major offensives.

In 1936 the Spanish Army was made up of two forces. One Army was based in Spain. It had 120,000 men, but they were poorly trained, and there was the Morocco-based Army of Africa. The Army of Africa numbered 34,000. It was battle-hardened from colonial conflicts and included well-disciplined Spanish Foreign Legion units. Italy provided 50,000 troops and 250 planes. The Germans provided a 'Condor Legion' of 19,000 soldiers plus the latest aircraft.

Tanks:

The use of Russian Soviet tanks in the Spanish Civil War provided examples of the potential and the problems of new military technologies. As the first significant use of armour since World War I, the Spanish Civil War was seen by some as showing valuable lessons in the debate over the future of tank warfare. In the case of the Soviet Red Army, the Spanish Civil War experience did have some critical consequences with tank technology, on the tactical side, many lessons were ignored, and many misunderstood.

The Spanish Civil War is regarded as a testing ground for the weapons and tactics of World War II. However, some caution must be used in assessing the lessons of the conflicts. The significance of the war for armoured warfare tactics has often been exaggerated, often based on misunderstandings of the size of the armoured forces employed and their goals. The Soviet-led tanks in Spain never attempted to prove or disprove theories of Blitzkrieg, deep battle, or trench warfare since the units involved were much too small to carry out such army-level or front-level operations. Nevertheless, Spain did provide some valuable lessons with technology, training, and tactics, some were appreciated, and many were not.

An American supporting the Republicans in the Spanish Civil War:

"Courage and heroism are plentiful in Spain, and the Spanish people have no lack of it. What they need are tactics."

In October 1936 a shipment of 50 Russian T-26 tanks and 51 volunteer tank specialists arrived. Due to the type of fighting taking place in Spain, the Russian T-26 was the primary type of tank sent to Spain 281 of the 331 tanks sent. The T-26 was not ideal for infantry support. It was lightly armoured, and vulnerable to contemporary anti-tank guns. The T-26 light tank required intermediate overhaul after 150 hours and a complete factory overhaul after 600 hours. The poor quality of the fuel damaged the engine to such an extent that it could immobilize the tank. Tracks (essentially the wheels of the tank) and track pins began to wear out after 500 miles of travel and clutches (devices to help change the gears) became worn out. In the end, trains started to be used to cut down the limited mileage of the tanks.

Co-operation between the tanks and the infantry was almost terrible, to begin with. This was due to there being no training with the tanks and infantry, and the tank units rarely worked with the same infantry unit for more than a few days, so no experience was accumulated. Radios were not used to link the infantry to the tanks, and the radios that they did have were not very useful. The infantry was slow, and the tanks fast, and the tanks were keen to move quickly because of anti-tank guns.

Brunete offensive

The Brunete offensive was a Republican plan intended to relieve Madrid with an attack that surrounded the defenders. It started from the west and the southeast of the capital, thus trapping the Nationalist forces. The attack by the Republicans began poorly. The tank battalion moved across an open field with the infantry following behind, but the tanks were stopped about half a kilometre from the town by the Nationalists using just two anti-tank guns and two field guns. Artillery and air support were requested. Four more attacks were unsuccessful to overcome resistance in the town. One of the German guns had been mounted in a church steeple and supposedly destroyed a dozen tanks. The town was finally taken by the Republicans, but they failed to reach their objectives on the first day. Over the following days, the tanks were used again but this time to support Republican infantry in a series of small local attacks, which also failed to fully dislodge the Nationalists. Even after committing their reserve tanks by July the Republicans had failed and were reduced to only 38 tanks.

Summary:

Tactically, it was like World War I without the extensive trench works and with better tanks and aeroplanes. In fact, the early part of the war saw WWI tanks in use. The officers on both sides were heavily influenced by French military tactics, which prized the offensive and the use of troops. Battles were head-on assaults for the most part. Fearlessness influenced the conduct of the individual soldier who at first scorned the use of cover and concealment. Even strongpoints were left uncamouflaged. The exception to this was the Moorish soldiers, who excelled at using cover.

All in all, it was a mess, devoid of tactics or strategy.

50 German tanks and men were sent but were not meant to fight and were considered volunteers. The German volunteers learnt that co-operation between infantry, tanks and plane was crucial.

Logistics and repairing were learnt.

They also captured Russian tanks, which they then used for the study.

The Soviet Union provided the Republicans with 1,000 aircraft and pilots, but Soviet knowledge was not as advanced as that of Germany.

The Republicans also employed deceptive tactics with help from the USSR. In addition to regular troops, Stalin sent Soviet advisers to train partisan guerrillas to make bombs and grenades, set ambushes, and carry out raids. Several years later, the Soviets would make use of guerrilla tactics developed during the Spanish Civil War in their defence of the USSR against the Nazis.

Submarines:

The emergence of submarines:

The first submarine was reported in 1562 in Spain.

Yet the British, French, Germans and Americans continued to develop these devices until the late 1800s.

The first military use of a submarine was during the American Civil War, 1861 – 1865.

Submarines/U-Boats, World War 1

U-Boat is an abbreviation of unterseeboot; when translated into English it means 'undersea boat'. When the First World War began, the Germans had 29 U-Boats available. Over a total of 4 months between October 1916 and January 1917, the Allies lost 1.4 million tons of shipping. Eventually, the Allied losses were reduced with the introduction of the convoy system in May 1917. These were merchant ships that were then encircled by military ships.

During WW1, Germany built 360 U-Boats, 178 of which were sunk. In total, they were responsible for the loss of more than 11 million tons of allied shipping. The British response to the increased losses was quick and relatively effective. Merchant's vessels were organised into convoys that were protected by the Royal Navy. A convoy is a group of ships, so instead of a boat operating on its own, they now worked as a group to protect each other. Safety in numbers!

By 1918, 200 ships had been sunk by 14 U-boats. U-boats eventually stopped surfacing because they too were suffering losses. Merchant ships would move together in large numbers under the defence of destroyers. The destroyers were fitted with hydrophones, which are underwater listening devices and depth charges; these are bombs that are launched from the surface ships and explode under water.

By June 1918, 16,539 ships had moved in convoys, and only 154 were hit, and more U-boats were sunk attacking convoys. Raids took place on U-boat bases in early 1918. The British also tried to block off the U-boat bases in German-occupied Belgium by sinking blockships at the harbour entrances. These had minimal success because they did not completely block off the entrances.

Submarines/U-Boats: World War 2

Submarine warfare developed during the Second World War. The Germans used wolf pack tactics. This meant that a group of U-boats, instead of a single U-boat, attacked Allied convoys and the escort vessels. To begin with, Allied shipping was unable to cope. The U-boats were very successful from 1940-42. The Allies were able to defeat this threat by developing better anti-U-boat tactics.

For example, they used aircraft fitted with radar sets to locate the U-boats under the sea and attack them. The most important reason was that the Allies were able to decode the German code system known as 'Enigma' and knew the location of the wolf packs. The Enigma code was broken due to the development of arguably the very first computer.

The wolf pack or Rudeltaktik in German had a devastating impact on Allied shipping. Despite only being implemented after the fall of France, the origins of this idea dated back to the First World War. (An example of continuity.)

This called for the development of a group of ships that would sail together as a group, under the protection of warships. Under the convoy system, the Germans could no longer find easy isolated targets. The U-boats that managed to find a convoy had difficulty attacking as it was escorted by antisubmarine vessels.

The British planned to build a defence area around their ships; the Germans were still operating their U-Boats independent of each other, and therefore it was uncoordinated. After France fell, the German commanders decided to form a group/pack of U-boats, they would delay an attack until they had enough submarines in position to attack as a group. This would hopefully overwhelm the escorts as the sheer number and surprise of the attacking boats would throw the convoy into confusion and possibly panic.

The first boat to make contact was called the shadower. It was their job to follow and to report the convoy's position back to the command submarine, the BdU (Befehlshaber der U-Boote). It would give orders to the other submarines. The shadower would remain out of sight of the convoy; it would be mainly submerged by day and then travelling on the surface by night. When enough boats had converged with the convoy, BdU would give the signal to attack, usually after dusk where the U-boats' small silhouette (outline of the ship) made detection difficult.

Now that the signal to attack had been given, each individual submarine was free to use any tactics. Some fired at long range, outside the area of the escorts, usually with a spread of several torpedoes. Some, particularly Otto Kretschmer (a German submarine commander), headed straight into the centre of the convoy and fired at point blank range. Whatever tactics were employed, the strategy was to attack by night, and then they would hide by day, with the attacks lasting several days, and more boats would arrive.

This had a devastating effect because attacking in groups would quickly overwhelm the escorts. When an escort pursued one U-boat, another would strike at a different location, creating total havoc.

Kretschmer later wrote in his war diary describing the attack on a convoy,

"The destroyers are at their wits' end. Shooting off star shells the whole time to comfort themselves and each other."

The Allies not only came up with arguably the world's first computer, Colossus, to break German codes, but they also brought in practical military technology and weapons.

They developed a shell that could light up the night sky on land and at sea called a star shell. The aim would be to use this at night to spot submarines.

Q-ships, also known as Q-boats, decoy vessels, special service ships, or mystery ships, were built. These were first used in 1915. A Q-ship looked like a harmless merchant ship but hid powerful guns. When a submarine surfaced, the guns would fire at the submarine.

Hydrophones were listening devices. They could hear a nearby submarine engine. Very well-organized in a convoy system, although not always successful in detecting U-boats.

Military Aircraft

Zeppelins

These were huge, hydrogen-filled airships that were used by the Germans as bombers. They were mostly large balloons, filled with hydrogen gas that would allow them to float, and they could be piloted with the use of propellers. The first Zeppelin raids hit British towns in 1915 and had a profound psychological effect on civilians who now no longer felt safe from the enemy. For the first time, civilians were directly attacked. However, apart from the psychological impact, the Zeppelins had limited impact because they could not carry enough bombs to cause severe damage.

In the end, the British government had to pull back fighter planes to defend Britain against these attacks.

The Germans used 130 Zeppelins of those 7 were lost to bad weather, 38 were lost in accidents, and 39 were shot down by the British.

Airships made about 51 bombing raids on England during World War One. These killed 557 and injured another 1,358 people.

Military aircraft – fighter and bomber planes.

Brigadier General Billy Mitchell, November 1918:

"The day has passed when armies on the ground or navies on the sea can be the arbiter of a nation's destiny in war. The main power of defence and the power of initiative against an enemy has passed to the air."

The first military conflict where aircraft were used in substantial numbers was World War One. At the beginning of the war, aircraft were only really used for scouting. As the war continued, technology also progressed, which allowed fighters and bombers to soar high over Western Europe. Interesting fact: Pilots at the start of the war would drop bricks on the enemy, which would then develop to bombs, as well as having machine guns attached.

Observation balloons had been employed in several wars and would be used to help artillery spot targets. Germany initially operated Zeppelins for scouting navy vessels in the North Sea and Baltic as well as for bombing raids over England and the Eastern Front.

Engineers and pilots learned from experience, leading to the growth of many specialized types of planes from fighters and bombers to ground-attack aeroplanes.

Military Aircraft Interwar years

The years between World War One and World War Two saw significant advancements in aircraft technology. Aeroplanes evolved from low-powered biplanes (wings on top and below) made from wood and fabric to sleek, high-powered monoplanes made of aluminium.

The first successful rotorcraft (a set or single propeller/propellers on the front of the plane) appeared in 1919; it was called the autogyro and was invented by Spanish engineer Juan de la Cierva.

Spanish Civil War:

The role of aircraft in the Spanish Civil War:

The Nationalist side conducted aerial bombing of cities in Republican territory, carried out mainly by the Luftwaffe volunteers of the Condor Legion and the Italian air force. Madrid, Barcelona, Valencia, Guernica, Durango, and other cities were attacked. The Bombing of Guernica was the most controversial and considered to be one of the world's first terror bombings. Terror bombing is an emotive term used for aerial attacks planned to weaken or break enemy morale.

July – September 1936:

The first significant airlift was conducted by the Nazi Legion Condor.

16,000 troops were brought from Spanish Morocco to mainland Spain.

March 1937: Battle of Guadalajara

Republican air units (mainly Soviet) struck Italian forces and caused them to retreat.

1937: Guernica

The German Luftwaffe's bombing of civilians was new to war and marked a new level of violence, demonstrated by the destruction of the city of Guernica in 1937.

The city had no direct involvement in the war and was 30 km from the battlefront.

There was an arms factory in the city.

The day of the bombing took place on the market day.

There were military battalions outside the city.

The city and the bridges were important targets for both cutting off the army on the frontier, and if the Nationalists wanted to take the capital, this would be an essential point to capture.

The attack gained controversy because it involved the bombing of civilians by a military air force. The offence started with incendiary bombs, and as people fled they were machine-gunned by fighter planes. It is estimated that 1,700 people were killed and 900 injured in the three-hour attack. It is difficult to say whether the Germans made this attack for strategic terror, or for a military strategic advantage. Experts in strategic bombing expected that direct attacks upon an enemy country's cities by bombers would lead to the quick collapse of civilian morale so that the people would put political pressure on the government to sue for peace leading to a general collapse.

March 1938: Barcelona

The Italians conducted a series of bombings on Barcelona, which caused about 2,000 causalities but did not cause the civilians to quit or the resistance to collapse. Quite the contrary, it hardened the civilians and unified them against the Nationalists.

Use of Aircraft in the 1934/1935-1936 Italo-Abyssinian War

(The Second Italo-Ethiopian war.)

Background

This was a conflict between Italy and Ethiopia .

Italy had had some foothold in the region since 1868, and Italians began to immigrate into the area. By the early 1900s Ethiopia and Liberia were the only two countries that had not been colonised by the European powers. Italy in the 1930s under Mussolini wanted to expand Italy's borders and Empire and considered Ethiopia to be territory worth gaining.

The conflict:

Many considered that the Ethiopians did not have the ability to fight back as they lacked industry, but various nations had given them substantial supplies, including the Nazi government, with 3 planes, 16,000 rifles, 600 machine guns and 10 million rounds of ammunition. The Italians had far more equipment, including aeroplanes, artillery, machine guns and tanks. They attacked from the East and from the South. The Ethiopians did manage some victories, and Benito Mussolini was impatient with the progress of his Italian army.

Ethiopia	Italy
Emperor Haile Selassie I	Benito Mussolini
Roughly 500,000 troops	Roughly 500, 000 troops
234 artillery	3,300 machine guns
300 trucks	275 artillery
7 armoured cars	200 tanks
4 Italian tanks	200 aircraft
13 aircraft (4 pilots)	

Use of gas

On December 26th, 1935, Mussolini ordered the use of chemical weapons and the destruction of villages. This was in response to the slow progress, the Christmas Day victory by the Ethiopians and claims of torture and execution of Italian prisoners of war. The Italians delivered the poison gas by aeroplane and artillery. The Ethiopians did not fully understand and appreciate the use of gas against them. In the first use of gas, the Ethiopians suffered 8,000 casualties. The aircraft had been equipped with special sprays, which would turn the chemicals into a rain-like substance, with enough aircraft being used that it was turned into a fog. This killed everything; not just the soldiers but also women, children, animals, and poisoned the land and rivers. The use of gas in battle and in the surrounding countryside caused the Ethiopians to switch tactics and begin a guerrilla offensive in April. By May 1936 the Italians had defeated the last Ethiopian armies, and both the southern and eastern Italian armies had met.

All of these wars indicated the increased importance of aircraft.

Military Aircraft WW2

Lessons had been learnt from the Spanish Civil War. World War II saw an increase in the production of aeroplanes and improvements to their weapons. Air combat tactics and doctrines took advantage (a doctrine is teachings in each branch of knowledge or belief system). Large-scale strategic bombing campaigns were launched, fighter escorts were introduced, and the more flexible aircraft and weapons allowed attacks on different targets with dive bombers, fighter-bombers, and ground-attack aircraft.

 This was furthered with new technologies such as radar to allow a more coordinated and controlled deployment of air defence.

While they first appeared during World War I, ground attack aircraft didn't provide a decisive contribution until the Germans introduced Blitzkrieg during the invasion of Poland and Battle of France, where aircraft functioned as mobile flying artillery to quickly disrupt defensive formations.

Artillery:

Artillery is a large weapon, designed to fire large ammunition over great distances. Built initially to destroy fortifications, during World War 1 their new aim was to destroy trench defences. Most attacks during World War I would start with an artillery bombardment that could last for days. This was aimed at destroying the enemy defences and fortifications, which would then allow the infantry to pass through into enemy territory.

Heavy artillery.

During WWI, artillery was heavily used. Attacks were rarely successful if they advanced beyond the range of its artillery. As well as bombarding the enemy in the trenches and attempting to cut the barbed wire, the artillery could be used to help infantry advances with a creeping barrage that mainly fired fragmentation (fragmentation means when the shell explodes it breaks up into tiny little pieces), high explosive, or with gas shells that appeared later in the war. The British experimented with firing thermite incendiary shells to set trees and buildings alight.

There were even cases of the two army's artillery firing directly at each other in an artillery battle.

One of the most significant issues for artillery during WWI was the production of ammunition. Both Allies and Entente had experienced shell shortages during the first year or two. This was due to both sides underestimating their importance and use during intense combat.

Artillery pieces were of two types: guns and howitzers.

Guns fired high-speed shells over a flat route and were often used to deliver fragmentation shells, which were meant to be able to cut through barbed wire.

Howitzers fired the shell high into the air, so it plunged into the ground. The largest calibres (the approximate internal diameter of the gun barrel, which gives you the width of the ammunition being fired) were usually howitzers. The Germans had a 420 mm howitzer, which weighed 20 tons and could shoot a one-ton shell over 10 km.

Firing:

1. The artillery would need to find a target using a person (observer) whose job was to find a target. This is partly why hot air balloons had been used in the past as they could see further.

Heavy Artillery WW2

During World War I, heavy artillery had been useful as long-range weapons. However, they were of little use against Blitzkrieg tactics employed by the German because Blitzkrieg moved too quickly for the artillery.

The heavy guns were used to protect essential harbours and coastal fortifications against attacks from the sea, but they were also unable to cope against modern warships and aircraft. As a result, the coastal batteries (a form of artillery designed to defend the coast) failed to defeat any massive attacks during World War Two.

The Germans spent large sums of money in improving long-range guns that could be used to shell mainland Britain from the French coast. Germany developed a heavy gun called the K12E also known as the Krupp. It started firing shells at Kent in 1940. However, it had no military significance and was abandoned soon afterwards. If you visit the town of Dover, you can see some of these shells today.

Field Artillery: WW2

Field Artillery are weapons used to support ground troops in battle.

During the Second World War, the major armies used the field gun and the field howitzer. The field gun could fire a light, high-velocity shell up to a range of about 15,000 yards.

The short-barrelled howitzer fired a heavier shell at a shorter distance.

Gas:

Early on in World War I, gases were used to attack. The aim would be to release the gas from cylinders in their own trench, with the hope that the wind would blow the gas at the enemy. This was generally unreliable, as they would only work if the direction of the wind was going in the direction of the enemy. Otherwise, it could blow back on the troops that fired them! Later, the gas was delivered by artillery or mortar shell.

There were three main gases used: mustard, chlorine, and phosgene.

In response, both sides developed gas masks.

Early on, improvised gas masks were made by urinating on a handkerchief, as the urea would disable the poison, the men would put the handkerchief over their mouth and nose!

Tear gas was first used in August 1914 by the French, but this only disabled the enemy. In April 1915, chlorine was used by Germany at the Second Battle of Ypres. A large dose could kill, but the gas was easy to detect by scent and sight. If you were not killed by being exposed, you could suffer permanent lung damage. Phosgene gas was first used in December 1915. It was the most lethal killing gas of World War One, 18 times more potent than chlorine and much harder to notice.

However, the most effective was mustard gas. It was introduced by Germany in July 1917. Mustard gas was hard to detect and stayed on the surface of the battlefield. In fact, 2% of mustard gas casualties died, mainly from another infection.

The main effect of gas was psychological. Soldiers on either side feared a gas attack. Yet the numbers of deaths compared to the numbers from the rest of the war only 3,000 British troops.

British use of gas in the Bolshevik Civil War.

In the winter of 1917, Vladimir Lenin and his Bolshevik party had staged a coup in Russia and had taken control over essential cities in Western Russia, including Moscow. The international community was shocked and scared by the new plans and a unique style of government being proposed by the Bolsheviks. In the summer of 1919, Britain and then secretary of state for war Winston Churchill suggested the idea of using chemical weapons on Bolshevik-controlled Russia. Churchill executed a sustained chemical attack on northern Russia.

"Gas is a more merciful weapon than [the] high explosive shell and compels an enemy to accept a decision with less loss of life than any other agency of war." Winston Churchill.

50,000 gas cylinders were shipped to Russia. British aerial attacks began using them in August 1919, targeting the village of Emtsa. It was reported that Bolshevik soldiers were seen fleeing as the gas moved towards them. The soldiers that were caught in the cloud vomited blood and then collapsed.

The attacks continued through September on many villages including Chunova, Vikhtova, Pocha, Chorga, Tavoigor and Zapolki. However, the weapons proved less effective than Churchill had hoped, partly because of the damp autumn weather. By September, the attacks were stopped.

British use of gas in Mesopotamia.

This period of history appears to be highly contentious. The historical view seems to be mixed; some sources suggest only tear gas was used and other historians have claimed it was tear gas and mustard gas. What we can say for sure was that tear gas was used and caused casualties. We can also say that the gas was considered for use, that the British had ordered the material, but it seems that the Royal Air Force had been reluctant to use the gas. Use of tear gas and lethal poison gas was promoted by Winston Churchill, head of the War Office:

"Gas is a more merciful weapon than high explosive shells and compels an enemy to accept a decision with less loss of life than any other agency of war. The moral effect is also very great. There can be no conceivable reason why it should not be resorted to. We have definitely taken the position of maintaining gas as a weapon in future warfare, and it is only ignorance on the part of the Indian military authorities which interposes any obstacle."

Martin Gilbert, Churchill and Bombing Policy, Fifth Churchill Lecture, Washington, D.C., 18 October 2005, http://xrl.us/bgy3j2

"It is odd that we do not use poison gas on these occasions." TE Lawrence, in The Observer 1920

Yet at the same time the historian Dr Robert Frisk maintains: *"in Iraq, Churchill urged the use of mustard gas, which had already been used against Shia rebels."* Robert Frisk, The Great War for Civilisation: The Conquest of the Middle East, London, 2006.

The British did bombard Shia rebels in the middle Euphrates with tear gas artillery shells, which supposedly were very useful in 1920.

From 1922 to 1925 it was also alleged that Kurdistan was bombed by the RAF using gas bombs, over disputes involving tribal armies or civilian populations.

From this period, we can see that the lessons were learnt and that even though Churchill had felt that this was a valuable weapon it was never used during World War II. Instead the RAF and Germans reverted to using other methods. As you can see, history can be a very blurred and murky set of events. Thus, the importance of a historian is to look at all sides of the arguments and evidence and come to a conclusion of your own, based on the evidence you have researched and read.

Japan vs the Soviet Union: Second Sino-Japanese War (1937-1945)

Background:

This was a conflict between Japan and the USSR. Tensions had been building along the Soviet and now Japanese borders. Japan had been expanding into China for years and had created a puppet state called Manchukuo. The new boundaries of the Japanese Empire bordered the Soviet Empire, and frictions began to increase with arguments over national boundaries. Skirmishes had taken place along Mongolia and Manchukuo. This has been termed an undeclared war, lasting from 1938 to 1939, which then rapidly escalated.

War Japan and the Soviet Union in 1939.

By the end of the year, the Japanese had brought 80,000 troops, 180 tanks and 450 aircraft into the battle.

Battle of Khalkhin Gol, 20 August 1939.

The battle started with an initial Japanese attack in July (July 2-25). The aim was to use a surprise attack to completely wipe out the Soviets. The Soviets suffered heavy losses compared to the Japanese, and only minor gains were made by the Japanese. Stubborn resistance and an armoured counter-blow stalled the Japanese attack. It turned into a stalemate with minor battles over the next weeks.

The Soviets then attempted some probing attacks in early August (August 7/8 and August 20), which were thrown back and gave them no territorial or logistical gains but did create considerable casualties. In the period between these three phases, the Soviets built up their forces, while the Japanese Army was ordered not to bring in reserves because of the fear of escalating the conflict.

Georgy Zhukov, and the beginnings of Russian war tactics.

Zhukov was a Russian commander for this area of warfare and had been with the Communists since 1918, fighting in many conflicts. He had an excellent understanding of combined attacks using tanks, infantry and aircraft, which he used during this battle.

Zhukov launched a successful counter-offensive in late August with a large force that planned to encircle the Japanese troops on the Soviet side of the river.

He commenced his operations with an artillery barrage, which would then be followed by tanks, supported by aircraft and bombers. At the beginning of the conflict, this appeared to be a typical conventional frontal attack. However, two groups of tanks, with artillery and infantry were held back. Their task was to attack the flanks of the Japanese army, with the aim of encircling them, and capturing their rear supplies. Within 11 days, the Japanese had been cleared from the border, giving the Soviets a clear victory.

This had enormous significance for the Soviet army, which would later be employed against the Germans in their attempted invasion of Russia.

This included the creation of underwater bridges, improving the cohesion, battle effectiveness of units and the development of the T-34 tanks, which were considered one of the best tanks of World War 2.

Japanese bombing of Manchuria (Shanghai).

"Words cannot express the feelings of profound horror with which the news of these raids had been received by the whole civilized world. They are often directed against places far from the actual area of hostilities. The military objective, where it exists, seems to take a completely second place. The main object seems to be to inspire terror by the indiscriminate slaughter of civilians..."

Lord Cranborne, The Illustrated London News, Marching to War 1933–1939, Doubleday, 1989, p.135

Background:

This was a conflict between Japan and China. The Japanese over the decades preceding the 1930s had been expanding their empire. They had moved into Korea and several islands in the Pacific.

To achieve these aims, the Japanese army had been modernised, and Japan had increased its army and Navy. Due to the failures of the Japanese military in the North of China with the Soviets, the Japanese government had decided to turn their attention south, inland to China and other islands in the Pacific. One of their first moves was to use the Army and Navy and coordinate the two together. The Japanese had an air force, but it was attached to the Army and Navy. It was not a separate organisation like the RAF.

The events in the bombing of Manchuria and Shanghai:

Manchuria is a state in China, and one of its largest cities is Shanghai. On the 23rd of August, the Japanese began the bombing Nanjing as well as other cities. The Chinese army of Shanghai arrived on the same day.

This was one of the first terror bombing campaigns in Asian, if not modern, history. Japanese assaults typically began at daybreak with the concentrated aerial bombing. Nevertheless, Japanese carrier aircraft bombed the city on 28 Jan 1932. It was the first significant aircraft carrier action in the Far East. Bombing efforts mostly targeted large Chinese cities such as Shanghai, Wuhan, and Chongqing, with roughly 5,000 air attacks from February 1938 to August 1943.

At midnight, Japanese carrier aircraft bombed Shanghai, in the first significant aircraft carrier action in East Asia. It was also arguably the first terror bombing of a civilian population of that era. The Japanese aircraft attacked causing 1,000 to 2,000 deaths, and roughly 3,000 injuries, most of which were civilian.

From August 15th to 18th, the Chinese fought the larger Japanese air force in intense air battles that saw two Japanese squadrons destroyed, including attacking the Japanese flagship Izumo.

The Japanese retaliated by launching raids on Shanghai. The Republic of China Air Force shot down six Japanese planes, suffering no losses.

However, China was not able to produce any planes of its own. Therefore, it was unable to replace damaged or destroyed aircraft. The aircraft that it did have were bought from abroad.

The Japanese had a good industrial and manufacturing process for their aeroplanes. They were also considered to be very capable of technologically advanced planes and could easily replace their losses. This was highlighted with both the Zero aeroplane, which the Americans did not have an answer for until they captured some of their downed planes and their invention of the jet engine.

It was therefore impossible for China to compete in an air war with Japan. In the Shanghai campaign, the Republic of China Air Force is said to have shot down 85 Japanese aeroplanes and sunk 51 ships, while losing 91 of its own aeroplanes, which was almost half of its air force.

Chapter 3:

The changing nature of sea warfare

***

World War 2 to Modern Day warfare.

This section will look at changing methods of naval warfare, from World War II to the Falklands War, including:

- Battle of the Atlantic
- Nuclear Submarines
- Aircraft Carriers
- Battle of the Pacific (including Pearl Harbour, Battle of the Coral Sea and the Battle for Midway)
- The Falklands Conflict

There were two important changes in naval warfare in the years following 1939:

1. Advances in submarines, with new U-boat tactics and the development of nuclear submarines.
2. Development of the aircraft carrier and it's use during the war in the Pacific and its development afterwards.

World War 2: Battle of the Atlantic

There were two phases to the Battle of the Atlantic:

1. German success in the years 1939-42.
2. The Second Phase: turning the tide.

German success in the years 1939-42:

Background:

This was a conflict between the Allies (mainly 🇬🇧 Britain and 🇺🇸 America) and 卐 Germany. Leading on from the Invasion of the Low land countries, a military campaign at sea started. From the start of the war the Germans knew the importance of cutting off American supplies to Britain, with the aim of starving Britain into submission.

This was described by the then British Prime Minister, Winston Churchill as the Battle of the Atlantic and he said:

"The only thing that ever really frightened me was the Battle of the Atlantic."

Events:

For three years, 1939 – 1942, German U-boats (also nicknamed 'iron coffins') were very successful and were close to victory. In 1940 the Germans sank 1,000 ships, which made up a ¼ of Britain's merchant fleet. By 1942, 1,661 Allied ships had been destroyed, and Britain was only able to import a third of the number of goods that it had imported in peacetime. By January 1943, the British navy had only two months' supply of oil left.

The Germans used a new tactic called 'wolf-pack'. They had also cracked the Allied codes, which meant that U-boats could lie in wait for Atlantic convoys and make co-ordinated attacks on them.

The British anti-U-boat tactics were not very useful, and they used out-of-date escort ships. British air cover was strong, but the planes were only able to travel some of the distance across the Atlantic Ocean. This still meant that there was a significant gap in the Atlantic where many U-boat attacks took place.

The German U-Boats also used the night to their advantage. By attacking from the surface and in the dark, the German U-boats were able to avoid detection by ASDIC, the British anti-submarine device which relied on soundwaves travelling through the water.

When the USA entered the war in December 1941, it gave U-boat commanders many more targets.

The Second Phase: Turning the Tide

From 1942, British Prime Minister Winston Churchill gave priority to beating the U-boat danger. The aim was to attack more U-Boats whilst reducing Allied shipping losses.

Between June and December of 1943, the Germans lost 141 U-boats while the Allies only lost 57 ships. The German U-boat commander Admiral Donitz was not able to replace the lost U-boats, and in March 1944 he called off the Battle of the Atlantic.

Reasons for Allied Success:

- Long range aircraft like the Liberator provided much-needed aerial protection to the convoys. This was further assisted using the Azores islands as Allied air bases, which closed the Atlantic gap by allowing continuous air support.

- The Allies decoded German radio messages, and so knew in advance the whereabouts of the U-boat packs. This was achieved with Alan Turing and his team, who invented what some call the first computer, to crack the code.

- Another critical factor was improved training for convoys and better-equipped escort vessels. These vessels were provided with the Hedgehog depth charge. The bomb would be fired from the boat, which went into the sea in clusters over a wide area and would sink into the sea and explode at different depths.

- The Allies were able to build ships faster than the U-boats could sink them.

1952: The birth of Nuclear Submarines:

Background:

Submarines underwent significant changes in the years after 1945, and the development of nuclear submarines played an essential role during the Cold War between the USA and the Soviet Union.

On January 21, 1952, the USA was the first to develop nuclear-powered submarines, with the launching of USS Nautilus. Within ten years, the Soviet Union had built their own version.

Nuclear submarines use nuclear technology rather than conventional air-breathing diesel engines.

What do you think is the immediate advantage of this?

Atomic powered submarines were armed with powerful nuclear weapons. Later, with the development of Cruise missiles gave submarines a long-range and robust ability to attack both on land and at sea. The submarines were equipped with cluster bombs to nuclear weapons. The British also developed their own nuclear submarines in the 1960s. They launched HMS Resolution in 1968, which carried Polaris missiles. This was later changed to the Trident missile system with the launching of HMS Vanguard in 1994.

It is important to take note that Nuclear submarines had advantages and disadvantages:

Disadvantages:

There were several accidents involving nuclear submarines. These were in part because of the dangers of operating underwater for long periods of time.

In 1963, the American Navy lost the nuclear submarine USS Thresher with 16 officers, 96 enlisted men and 21 civilians on board. While 220 miles east of Boston, USA the USS Thresher went to sea at 6:30 am and it had disappeared by 11:30 am. It reported problems through a garbled transmission and then went silent. This is considered to the be the deadliest submarine disaster in history.

In 2000, the Russian submarine Kursk sank during military training exercises, with the loss of 118 crew members. The submarine was believed to have been destroyed by an explosion caused by a torpedo, that led to a further set of detonations, which killed all the crew.

It is impossible to put nuclear submarines on silent running as the nuclear reactor (engine) needs to be kept switched on. This is a disadvantage when compared to submarines with diesel engines, which can be switched off, allowing those submarines to operate in silence.

Advantages:

Nuclear submarines have many benefits over diesel submarines. They do not need to come to the surface as frequently, as they are able to refilter their air.

Compared to a conventional submarine engine, the power generated by the nuclear reactor is vast. The reactor can run the submarine at high speeds for long and nonstop periods of time and do not require refuelling intervals as they can operate underwater throughout their lifetime. Due to their stealth, they can force an enemy navy to waste their resources in searching vast areas of ocean and protecting ships against attack.

Nuclear submarines have been important in numerous conflicts:

- The Falklands War (1982) a British atomic submarine sank an Argentine cruiser
- The first Gulf War (1991) when submarines were used to launch Tomahawk Cruise Missiles at strategic land targets inside Iraq.

The aircraft carrier:

The creation of the aircraft carrier was the most crucial development in naval warfare, both during and after the Second World War. The aircraft carrier was to play an essential role in several wars in the second part of the 20th century, including the Falklands War in 1982, and the first Gulf War in 1991.

A timeline of key developments in the aircraft carrier: 1912-1923:

1912 - Lieutenant Charles Santon flew a biplane off a platform constructed on a stationary battleship.

1914-18 - HMS Furious was converted into an aircraft carrier with a small runway (Known as a take-off the deck). A plane did manage to land on the carrier but after the landing fell over the side and killed the pilot.

1918 - HMS Furious successfully launched six aircraft.

1922 - The Japanese designed the first aircraft carrier, Hosho.

1923 - The first specially made British aircraft carrier, Hermes.

Further detail: Timeline of key developments in the aircraft carrier: 1940-1970

* **1940**

During World War 2, aircraft carriers played an essential role in the Battle of Taranto. Aeroplanes known as Swordfish took off from the aircraft carrier, HMS Illustrious, and attacked the Italian fleet at the port of Taranto. The Swordfish flew 250 kilometres and damaged or destroyed three Italian battleships and ended Italy as a naval power. The battle was noticed by the Japanese, who saw the success and used similar methods at Pearl Harbor. Then, in the 1940s the slanted deck was introduced, which gave carriers two runways from which to conduct operations.

* **1960**

1961 saw the first nuclear-powered aircraft carrier, which was named the USS Enterprise. This had 5,000 crew and carried over 100 jet aircraft.

* **1970**

In the 1970s, Nimitz-class aircraft carriers were developed, which are supercarriers with an overall length of 333 metres. They are the largest capital (lead or main ship in a fleet) ships in the world.

Now into the detail:

Since World War II, aircraft carrier designs have increased in size to accommodate a steady increase in aircraft size. The large, modern Nimitz class of US carriers has a displacement (weight) nearly four times that of any World War II-era submarine. However, its number of aircraft is roughly the same. This is a consequence of the steadily increasing size and weight of military aircraft over the years.

Modern navies that operate such aircraft carriers treat them as the capital ship of the fleet, a role previously held by the battleship. The change in importance took place during World War II and was in response to air power becoming an essential factor, driven by the superior range, flexibility and effectiveness of carrier-launched aircraft.

Following WW2, carriers continued to increase  in size and importance. Supercarriers, which can displace 75,000 tonnes or more, have become the pinnacle of carrier development. Some are now powered by nuclear reactors.

What might be a downside of having a nuclear-powered aircraft carrier, while at war?

Amphibious landings:

Amphibious landings are led by assault ships. Their aim is to carry and land troops as well as having many helicopters for that purpose. They are known as 'commando carriers' or 'helicopter carriers', many can operate VSTOL aircraft (a vertical and short take-off and landing, like the British Harrier).

Not having the firepower of other warships, carriers are considered vulnerable to attack by other ships, aircraft, submarines, or missiles. Therefore, an aircraft carrier is generally accompanied by some other vessels to protect the relatively cumbersome carrier, to carry supplies and perform other support services, and to provide additional offensive capabilities. The resulting group of boats is often termed a battle group, carrier group, or carrier battle group.

Battle of the Pacific, 1941-45

Background:

This was a war between the ▬ USA and ※ Japan, which highlighted the importance of aircraft carriers in naval conflicts. Control of the vast Pacific Ocean and the islands contained within it was dependent on air power. US and Japanese aircraft carriers played a decisive role in several battles.

Isoroku Yamamoto (1884 – 1943) was a Japanese Marshal Admiral and the commander-in-chief of the Combined Fleet during World War II.

Chester Nimitz (1885 – 1966) was a fleet admiral of the United States Navy. He played a significant role in the naval history of World War II as Commander in Chief of the United States Pacific Fleet.

Conflicts:

Pearl Harbor, December 1941.

Background:

This was the first conflict of World War Two between Japan and the USA. On the 7th of December 1941, the US Pacific Fleet at Pearl Harbor was attacked by the Japanese.

President Franklin D. Roosevelt proclaimed December 7, 1941, to be *"a date which will live in infamy."*

Events:

The Japanese sent a strike force that used 60 planes and bombers for the attack. Although considerable damage and casualties were inflicted on the US fleet. The attack was not decisive because all of America's Pacific aircraft carriers were not in port on that day. There were four in total at the time.

The attack had several important aims. The overall objective was for Japan to conquer Southeast Asia without interference.

It intended to destroy crucial American ships, including battleships and aircraft carriers. The Japanese believed that this would prevent the Pacific Fleet from interfering with their conquest of the Dutch East Indies and Malaya.

It was thought that this action would give time for Japan to strengthen its position and increase its naval strength, before shipbuilding authorised by the 1940 Vinson-Walsh Act erased any chance of victory.

It was meant to deliver a blow to American confidence, one which would discourage Americans from committing to war in the western Pacific Ocean and Dutch East Indies. To maximise the effect on morale, battleships were chosen as the primary targets, since they were the prestige ships of any navy.

All 8 U.S. Navy battleships were damaged, and four were sunk. The Japanese also sank and damaged three cruisers, three destroyers, an anti-aircraft training ship, and one minelayer. 188 American aircraft were destroyed, 2,403 Americans were killed and 1,178 others were wounded. Essential base installations such as the power station, shipyard, maintenance and fuel and weapon warehouse buildings, as well as the submarine bases and headquarters building. This building was to be the home of the intelligence section and was not attacked.

Japanese losses were small: 29 aircraft and five midget submarines were lost, and 64 members of the armed forces killed. One Japanese sailor, Kazuo Sakamaki, was captured.

Admiral Hara Tadaichi said later, *"We won a great tactical victory at Pearl Harbor and thereby lost the war."*

The Japanese belief in their ability to achieve a short, successful war meant that they did not attack the navy repair yards, oil tank farms, submarine base and old headquarters building. All these targets were excluded, yet they proved more important than any battleship to the American war battles in the Pacific.

The continuation of the repair shops and fuel depots allowed Pearl Harbor to maintain logistical support to the US Navy's operations, such as the Battles of the Coral Sea and Midway.

It was submarines that immobilised the Imperial Japanese Navy's massive ships and brought Japan's economy to a virtual standstill. They paralysed the transport of oil and raw materials: the import of raw materials was below half of what it had been at the end of 1942, to a disastrous ten million tons, while oil imports were almost completely stopped.

Lastly, the bunker of the Old Administration Building was the headquarters of the code-breaking department, which contributed to the Midway ambush and the American section of submarines achieving victory.

The Battle of the Coral Sea.

Background:

This was a battle between the USA, Australia and Japan. The battle took place in early May 1942. The US code-breaking department decoded Japanese messages. This allowed the Americans to plan and prepare an aircraft carrier fleet to intercept the Japanese navy. The battle was the first engagement in which aircraft carriers attacked each other, as well as being the first time neither side's ships saw or fired directly at each other. During the battle, the Japanese lost two and the USA one aircraft carrier.

Events:

On 3–4 May, Japanese forces successfully attacked and seized Tulagi. However, several of their warships were surprised and sunk or damaged by aircraft from the US carrier Yorktown.

The Japanese fleet carriers pushed towards the Coral Sea with the purpose of locating and defeating the Allied naval forces.

On the 7th May, carrier forces from both sides fought for two days. On the first day, the US sank the Japanese light carrier Shōhō, while the Japanese sank a US destroyer and damaged a fleet oiler. The next day, the Japanese carrier Shōkaku was destroyed, the US fleet carrier Lexington was damaged so severely that it was scuttled and the Yorktown was damaged. With both sides having experienced substantial losses in aircraft and carriers, the two fleets left the battle area. Due to the loss of carrier air cover Japanese ships were recalled.

It was a tactical victory for the Japanese because of the number of American ships sunk. The battle proved to be a significant success for the Allies for several reasons:

The Japanese aircraft carriers Shōkaku and Zuikaku had been severely affected. One was damaged and the other had a reduced number of aircraft. Both carriers were therefore unable to engage in the Battle of Midway, which took place the next month, ensuring a roughly equal number of aircraft between the two adversaries and contributing significantly to the US victory in that battle.

The battle was the first time since the start of the war that the Japanese progress had been halted by the Allies.

The Battle of Midway.

Background:

This was a battle between the USA and Japan in June 1942. This is considered the most decisive naval battle of the Second World War. After Pearl Harbour, Admiral Yamamoto decided to try and capture the US base on Midway Island. He believed that the Japanese Air Force would be able to launch air attacks on the US Fleet at Pearl Harbour. Once again, US codebreakers broke Japanese codes and knew of their plans and were able to intercept the Japanese carrier fleet.

Events:

Before the war started, Japanese Admiral Yamamoto devised an elaborate scheme whereby the Combined Fleet was broken into eight task groups. Two of these groups made a diversionary assault on the Aleutian Islands. The rest of the fleet was led by Yamamoto and headed for Midway.

Unknown to Yamamoto, the US intelligence service had broken the Japanese communication code and informed Admiral Chester Nimitz of the Japanese plans. Nimitz assembled two task forces, including the carriers Yorktown, Enterprise and Hornet, eight cruisers, and fifteen destroyers, they also headed for Midway.

On 3rd June 1942, 100 aircraft bombed Midway. The US Marine fighters were outnumbered and were unable to stop the extensive damage being caused. American carrier-based planes turned the tide. They had a lot of luck; they found and attacked that the Japanese aircraft whilst they were being rearmed.

During the battle, US dive bombers sank three Japanese aircraft carriers and severely damaged a fourth.

Torpedo bombers became separated from the American dive-bombers and were slaughtered (36 of 42 shot down), but they diverted Japanese defences just in time for the dive-bombers to arrive; some of them had become lost, and now by luck, they found the Japanese. The Japanese carriers were caught while refuelling and rearming their aircraft, which made them defenceless.

The Americans destroyed 4 fleet carriers, which was the entire strength of the task force. This included the Akagi, Kaga, Soryu, and Hiryu, which had 5,0000 sailors and 322 aircraft. The Japanese also lost the heavy cruiser Mikuma.

The American casualties included 147 aircraft and more than three hundred seamen.

Although the US lost an aircraft carrier, the battle was an important turning point in the war in the Pacific.

Analysts often point to Japanese aircraft losses at Midway as eliminating the power of the Imperial Navy's air forces but, in fact, about two-thirds of aircrews survived. More disastrous was the loss of qualified mechanics and ground crews who went down with the ships. Some historians see Midway as the turning point in the Pacific theatre of war, after which the Americans rode straight to Tokyo; others view it as a cusp in the war, after which the initiative hung in the balance. It gave the USA control of the sea and the air. This would then give them several advantages, including disabling the Japanese war supplies heading for Japan and allowing the Americans to begin the tactic of island-hopping, freeing islands from the Japanese, to swing toward the Allies in the Guadalcanal campaign. Either way, Midway ranks as a genuinely decisive battle.

The Falklands War, 1982

Background:

This was a war between Britain and Argentina. In April 1982, Argentina had invaded the Falkland Islands, which were based in the South Atlantic and ruled by the British. However, these islands were thousands of miles away from the U.K., so they had to build a U.K. task force and send it to the Falklands, 3000 miles away. This conflict illustrated the importance of naval power in deciding the outcome of a war. It emphasised the importance of the submarine and the aircraft carrier.

The battle was an episode over the sovereignty of this territory. Argentina stated (and maintains) that the islands were Argentinian territory, and the Argentine government thus characterised its military action as the reclamation of its territory. The British government regarded the move as an invasion of a region that had been a British colony since 1841. Falkland Islanders, who have populated the islands, are mainly descendants of British settlers and favour British sovereignty.

Events:

Argentina attacked the islands on 2 April 1982, using special forces, which landed at Mullet Creek and advanced. They found little opposition; the island only contained fifty-seven British marines and eleven sailors, as well as the Falkland Islands Defence Force. There was only one Argentine death. The event earned international attention at a level which the islands had never experienced before and made the Falklands a household name in the UK. The British responded with an expeditionary force that landed seven weeks later Government House in Stanley, with a secondary force coming in from Yorke Bay.

The UK sent a task force, which included two aircraft carriers: Invincible and Hermes. Due to their importance, the aircraft carriers would be important targets for Argentine submarines. The carriers had Sea Harriers. They protected British troops landings when they landed on the islands and attacked Port Stanley.

During the conflict, the British nuclear-powered submarine HMS Conqueror sank the Argentine cruiser General Belgrano. The Argentine Navy realised that they had no adequate defence against submarine attack and the Argentine surface fleet retreated to port for the remainder of the war, though an Argentine submarine remained at sea. After the battle, it was revealed that the Argentines had fired six torpedoes, but none had hit their targets.

After intense combat, the Argentine garrison quit on 14 June 1982. The war proved to be an exception in some different respects.

The Falklands conflict remains the largest air-naval combat operation between modern armies since the Second World War. As such, it has been the subject of serious study by military analysts and historians. The most critical lessons discovered include the vulnerability of surface ships to anti-ship missiles and submarines, the difficulties of arranging logistical support over a long-distance, and reconfirmation of the role of tactical air power, including the use of helicopters. Not least, the Falklands conflict also proved that small arms still had a role to play.

Timeline of the Falklands War of 1982:

April 2nd: Argentinean forces invaded the Falkland Islands.

April 3rd: Argentinean troops occupied South Georgia.

April 12th: Britain announced a 200-mile Exclusion Zone around the Falkland Islands.

May 1st: Task Force entered the Exclusion Zone. Vulcan bomber 'Black Buck' attacked the runway at Port Stanley. First air attacks by Harriers on Argentinean positions on the Falklands. SAS landed on the islands.

May 2nd: 'General Belgrano' sunk by 'HMS Conqueror'.

May 4th: The destroyer 'HMS Sheffield' was hit by an Exocet missile. 20 men were killed. First Harrier lost over Goose Green.

May 12th: 'HMS Glasgow' disabled by an Argentine bomb.

May 21st: 'HMS Ardent' lost.

May 23rd: 'HMS Antelope' lost.

May 25th: 'HMS Coventry' lost; 'HMS Broadsword' damaged; 'Atlantic Conveyor' hit by an Exocet missile.

June 14th: Argentine forces on the Falkland Islands surrendered.

July 13th: Argentine government accepts an end to hostilities.

Summary of changes and continuity:
Changes:

Submarines (Nicknamed Iron coffins.)

The shift from diesel to nuclear power allows nuclear submarines to travel longer distances underwater as nuclear-powered engines do not require oxygen. However, diesel engines could be switched off, so they could be quieter.

Modern submarines are now capable of firing at targets on land. In this war they operated from both the Red Sea and the Arabian Gulf, U.S. submarines fired over 1/3 of over 800 Tomahawks launched by naval forces during the conflict.

Aircraft Carriers

They have increased in size. The large, modern Nimitz class of U.S.N. carriers has a displacement (which reflects the displacement of water, to give you an idea of scale) of nearly four times that of the World War II-era USS Enterprise.

Aircraft carriers now have nuclear reactors. USS Enterprise was the first aircraft carrier. Construction started in 1958, it was launched in 1961 and used until 2012.

Aircraft carriers are now used for sea and land operations and were involved in these operations in the First and Second Gulf Wars.

Since 1989, carriers have been designed to be used in amphibious landing operations.

Continuity:

Submarines

Able to attack sea targets, and this is still their primary function. Submarines have been used from WWII to the Falklands War and the sinking of Belgrano by HMS Conqueror. HMS Conqueror is the only nuclear submarine to have attacked an enemy ship with torpedoes.

Submarines have been used to protect merchant vessels from the Battle of the Atlantic in WW2 to the First and Second Gulf War and are still used today for this purpose.

Aircraft carriers

Still used for their primary function as a naval mobile air base.

They became the lead ship or capital ship of the Navy during WW2, which continued during the First and Second Gulf Wars and is still the case today.

Anti-submarine warfare:

German U-boats primarily completed operations on the surface and were limited in how much they could go underwater.

Active Sonar was developed from the hydrophone system used in World War 1 (sound navigation and ranging). Sonar sends out sound waves that bounce back if they hit a solid object. There were limits to this technology as this was only effective at slow speed and if the enemy ship was not too close. The closer the enemy vessel the harder it was to find using sonar. Finally, the sonar could only detect U-boats if they were submerged; if they were on the surface, which most of the U-boats would be during the attack, they could not be detected.

Hunter Killer Groups: These were escort carriers, that contained carriers and destroyers. The planes were equipped with bombs, depth charges and homing torpedoes. They could patrol vast areas for several hours.

A depth charge is a high explosive charge that is designed to explode at a certain depth. These were available in World War 1 and then improved for World War 2. Submarines in World War 2 were more resistant to these because of better manoeuvrability and welded hulls. Improvements were made, adding weights, bigger explosives and changing and varying the depth for the explosion. There were other improvements with the Squid and Hedgehog, which were launched like a mortar.

Airborne radar (Radio Detection and Ranging): At the beginning of the war they were limited in number and reliability. However, as the war progressed, they were effective at detecting during bad weather or at night, which is when most attacks took place.

Searchlights were used in the battle of the Atlantic with aircraft. The aircraft would fly over the water and point the searchlight on the surface of the sea to catch submarines on the surface of the sea.

High-frequency direction finding is a type of radio direction finder (RDF) introduced in World War II.

The total combat loses of Submarines in WW2, were 757, around 250 were sunk by aircraft and 40 by aircraft and ships working together.

Chapter 4:

Nature of Land Warfare during WW2

***

This chapter will look at different forms of combat on land, in particular:

1. World War Two tactics
2. Middle Eastern conflicts
3. Guerrilla Warfare tactics
4. Civilian resistance movements

This section will look at methods of warfare on land during World War 2:

- Blitzkrieg
- Invasion of Poland
- Invasion of the Low Countries and France
- Operation Barbarossa
- Battle of the Bulge

Weird Fact: If you know about Santa's sleigh and his reindeer, you will understand that Donner and Blitzen are two of the reindeer. Their names mean Thunder and Lightning.

Blitzkrieg means Lightning War – it was a coordinated attack using both ground troops and air force working together to hit targets.

Blitzkrieg was an innovative military system first employed by the Germans during World War Two and was a tactic based on speed and surprise. It was created by Alfred von Schlieffen; thus the name 'Schlieffen Plan.' This was a doctrine formed during WWI that focused on quick military victory. Blitzkrieg relied on a military based around light tank units supported by planes and infantry.

Later, a German officer called Heinz Guderian looked at new weapons and vehicles including dive bombers and light tanks, with the aim of improving the German army's manoeuvrability.

German Major General Fuller said that *"Speed, and still more speed, and always speed was the secret.......and that demanded audacity, more audacity and always audacity."*

As a tactic, it was employed to devastating effect in the opening years of World War Two and caused the British and French armies to be forced back over just a few weeks to the beaches of Dunkirk. It was also central to the German army's destruction of Russian forces when they attacked Russia in June 1941.

Aircraft, paratroopers, tanks, vehicles, cavalry and finally infantry.

Stage 1:

First, the Luftwaffe (German Airforce) would come up with a strategic target and use Stuka dive bombers to attack airfields and communications targets, including power lines, phone lines, bridges, roads and railway tracks that were surrounding the strategic objective.

As the Stukas completed their task the German tanks were advancing, and the planes would retire just at the last minute so that the enemy would not have time to recover before the tanks attacked, supported by infantry.

Stage 2:

Then the army would move in using tanks, motorbikes and armoured cars.

This meant that they could break through the lines quickly and attack the enemy and their critical targets. Moreover, one of the significant successes of the Blitzkrieg was its adoption of FM radios. The communication technology allowed for quick, decentralised decision-making that was key to this speed-focused tactic. When the tanks that had broken through the enemy lines, they could also use the radios to inform support units as to their progress, location and what enemy forces they had encountered.

Blitzkrieg Summary

It meant 'lightning war' and was created to achieve a quick victory and avoid another stalemate such as that encountered on the Western Front during the First World War. Blitzkrieg practised shock tactics with the purpose being to paralyse the opponent by destructive use of the most up-to-date technology.

Airpower was used to bombard enemy airfields and communications and slow down their response to the Blitzkrieg attack.

↓

The Germans purposely struck a weak spot in the enemy defences

↓

This attack was conducted with supreme force and speed by motorised vehicles, tanks and air power, especially dive bombers known as Stukas

↓

The attack was coordinated by radio

↓

Reinforcements would then follow and secure the area.

Poland:

Background:

This was a battle between Germany, Poland and the USSR. Germany had decided to invade Poland and had made a strategic alliance with Russia to attack Poland together, on two sides. Hitler wanted to expand German territory to the East and eventually the whole of Europe. Germany had already grown into Austria and Czechoslovakia at this point. Poland was the next stage.

Events:

Poland was invaded by Germany on September 1st, 1939. The Germans code-named the Operation White (Fall Weiss). The attack on Poland began at 4.45 a.m. when a Blitzkrieg attack ripped through the Polish army. Within a month Poland had capitulated to the Germans, and the country was defeated.

How did Germany win so easily?

The Germans had been developing new strategies, refining old ones, building in old tactics and building new fighting vehicles to implement them. The Polish Army, like many others in Europe, had stayed with a World War One mentality.

No-one doubts that the Polish army put up an intense fight, but they were the first army to feel the full force of Blitzkrieg. Tanks versus a fundamentally non-mechanised army could only lead to one result: Cavalry vs Tanks could only lead to one conclusion, no matter how brave the Polish soldiers were.

Many of the German tanks were equipped with machine guns or small calibre guns, compared to later tank designs. The real damage came because of the constant barrage of all parts of Blitzkrieg, which included large numbers of tanks as well as support vehicles and aircraft. This stopped the Polish Army from re-grouping.

There was also the fact that the Germans had complete air superiority which meant that it was even harder for the retreating Poles to regroup and fleeing civilians did a great deal to prevent a controlled withdrawal by the Polish military.

According to Heinz Guderian: *"On September 5th our corps had a surprise visit from Adolf Hitler. I met him near Plevno on the Tuchel-Schwetz road, got into his car, and drove with him along the line of our previous advance. We passed the destroyed Polish artillery, went through the Schwetz, and then, following closely behind our encircling troops, drove to Graudenz, where he stopped and gazed for some time at the blown bridges over the Vistula. At the sight of the smashed artillery regiment, Hitler had asked me: "Our dive-bombers did that?" When I replied, "No, our Panzers!", he was astonished."*

The Low Countries and France, May 1940

Background:

This was a battle between Germany, Holland, Belgium, France and Britain. On the 10th of May, the Germans attacked Belgium and Holland. Both nations were no match for the Germans. It took five days to break Holland, who capitulated after a massive bombing raid on Rotterdam. On the 12th of May, the Germans invaded France through the woodlands of the Ardennes in Belgium. The German troops quickly crossed the River Meuse and outflanked the British and French armies. On 21st June, the French surrendered.

In 1939, as World War Two approached, the British and French planned to fight an updated version of what happened during World War One, but with some significant differences. The French had experienced massive casualties in frontal assaults in World War One. This time they planned to stay on the defensive while preparing their military forces and industrial base to fight a total war. They then aimed to take the offensive within two to three years after the start of hostilities.

The 'Maginot Line' replaced the crude trenches with a sophisticated series of fortifications, which were expected to protect France's frontier with Germany. However, the line did not cover the Franco-Belgian border.

By May 1940, Europe had been in World War Two for nine months. Despite this, Britain and France had seen little real fighting, with some advances into Germany, but this was in part because the Allies were still hoping for a peaceful resolution.

Events:

Hitler was keen to follow up his victory over Poland in 1939 by attacking in the west, but poor weather forced the planned offensive to be suspended. In January 1940, a German plane crash landed in Belgium, with a copy of the attack orders on board.

As a result, Hitler was required to reconsider the military's plan. He turned to General Erich von Manstein, who argued for a daring campaign. Manstein predicted that the Maginot Line was too complicated for a direct attack from Germany. Instead, he proposed another route for the attack. Through neutral Holland and Belgium, with the central thrust against France to be started a little later through the Ardennes. The Ardennes was a rugged and densely forested region on the German-Belgian-French border, where the Allies would be unlikely to expect an attack. The plan was to rely heavily on Blitzkrieg.

The tanks were assembled into armoured (Panzer) groups. The French had some formations that were as good, but they had been spread out over the areas of Northern France instead of having been placed in groups.

Manstein's planned for the Panzer groups to have a semi-independent role. They would race ahead of the central part of the army, with the aim of punching holes in weak points as well as disrupting and disorientating the Allies. This was a dangerous plan and was opposed by some generals. Hitler did have some misgivings but still gave his approval.

The assault began on the 10th of May 1940, with German air raids on Belgium and Holland followed by parachute drops deep inside enemy territory, whilst armoured divisions began moving into Belgium, Holland and France. Holland and Belgium allied with France and Britain, but this only complicated the Allied command and control arrangements further.

The Germans seized the initiative, capturing the critical Belgian fort of Eban Emael with a small airborne operation. The pace of the German advance and the air raids gave the Germans a huge psychological advantage and by the 14th of May the Dutch surrendered.

The German plan of attack through the Ardennes Forest, code-named Case Yellow, aimed to break through to the south of the British and then split them from the French in the South.

The British and French had responded by putting into operation a plan to advance to Belgium. The Allies pushed their best forces into Belgium, which started well until the French army advancing towards Holland was pushed back by German forces.

Soon it became clear that by advancing into Holland and Belgium the Allies were playing into Hitler's military plan. On the 13th of May, the first German forces emerged from the Ardennes. The fighting lasted two days as the Panzers crossed the river near the Ardennes. Despite stiff resistance from the under-equipped French defenders, and near-suicidal attacks by Allied aircraft, the Germans broke through.

The German attack quickly destroyed Dutch forces, and the bombing of Rotterdam persuaded the Netherlands to surrender on 15 May. Although German troops in the north encountered strong French and Belgian resistance, the leading German thrust through the Ardennes was an enormous achievement.

French divisions were not prepared or equipped to deal with the significant armoured thrust that developed and were hammered by constant attacks by German bombers.

Just four days into the attack German troops had burst through the French lines. The Allies attempted counter-attacks by air and land, but they failed with heavy losses. In part, this was happened due to the speed of events. The (B.E.F.) British Expeditionary Force, with the best units of the French army, was still in the north and had seen little fighting. The Germans had broken through to the south and now forced some of the French forces and all the British in the North to retreat to avoid being cut off. On the 20th of May, German tanks reached Amiens and trapped the British and French troops in the North. They now made for Dunkirk to evacuate to England.

The British put a last-minute evacuation plan into a place known as 'Operation Dynamo'. Between the 26th of May and the 4th of June Hitler halted the German advance on Dunkirk, allowing 200,000 British and 140,000 French soldiers to be evacuated to England.

On the 5th of June, the Germans swung south and the French army finally collapsed, although not without heavy fighting. The French Government surrendered on the 25th of June, just seven weeks after the beginning of the invasion.

Reasons for Allied failure and German success.

- ➢ Lack of preparation. The British and French had no preparations to deal with Maginot despite the lessons of Poland.

- ➢ Surprise. The French and British did not expect the Germans to attack through the Ardennes because of it being a heavily wooded area that they believed was unsuitable for tanks.

- ➢ Speed. The Blitzkrieg assault took the British and French by surprise due to the speed of the attack and allowed the Germans to outflank and split the British and French armies.

- ➢ Belgian neutrality, and Dutch neutrality until they were invaded by the Germans, caused significant problems with planning, including the incompletion of the Maginot line. It also meant that during the fighting there had been no co-ordination systems put in place for the four nations, made even harder to organise in the heat of battle.

Operation Barbarossa: Blitzkrieg in the Soviet Union, 1941-42

Background:

Hitler, *"We have only to kick in the door, and the whole rotten structure will come crashing down."*

Stalin, *"Hitlers come and go, but Germany and the German people remain."*

This was a conflict between Germany and the USSR during World War Two. Germany and the USSR was an almost inevitable conflict; two dictators with different ideologies, and they both loathed each other. Stalin hated any form of Capitalism and Hitler hated Communism. The two sides had shown some cooperation, and they had come into conflict. Hitler decided that a pre-emptive strike was the way forward and Stalin stalled for time to get the USSR ready to fight a war. This would be one of the most significant conflicts of the war, and a near struggle to the death.

Weird Fact:

More deaths occurred in the first week of fighting in Operation Barbarossa than all the deaths of the Vietnam War.

Events:

The planning for Operation Barbarossa had begun over a year beforehand, in the wake of Germany's stunning success against the western allies in France. The triumphalism that followed this victory, combined with widely believed reports that the Soviet armed forces were weak and deficient (evidenced by defeats by Finland in 1939) led to high optimism among the German high command.

In June 1941, German troops invaded the Soviet Union. Blitzkrieg was effective in the first year, but it eventually failed in Russia. It was a three-pronged invasion with the aim of capturing Leningrad in the North, Moscow in the centre and Stalingrad and the valuable oil area of the Caucasus to the South. The German armies pushed quickly with Soviet troops throughout in retreat. By September they were close to Leningrad in the North and Moscow in the centre. This initial victory was due to several factors:

1) Speed. The speed of the German attacks coupled with the surprise of the attack meant that the Russians were not prepared.

2) Lack of preparation. Stalin, the Soviet leader, had made few plans for such an invasion, in part because he felt that this could provoke Hitler into invading. He had severely decreased the effectiveness of his armed forces by removing senior officers during his purges of the late 1930s. Due to the Soviet invasion of Poland, the Soviet army had to create new defences, which were not completed in time.

3) Air superiority. The Luftwaffe secured command of the air and was able to support the German progress.

The attack started at 03.00 on June 22nd, 1941. In total, the Germans and their allies had 3 million soldiers, 3580 tanks, 7184 artillery guns, 1830 planes and 750,000 horses.

By Day 17, 300,000 Russians had been taken, and 2,500 tanks, 1,400 artillery guns and 250 aircraft were seized or destroyed. This was only in the area invaded by the Army Group Centre. The Russian Army looked as if it was on the brink of a total collapse, and Moscow seemed fated to fall.

In fact, the German advance had been so fast that it had compromised the whole of their army's lines of supply and communication. The Army Group Centre rested on the Desna, but it was still thought that they were only catching their breath before moving on. Nevertheless, it was now that the German army was jeopardised by Hitler. Guderian was infuriated by this order.

Hitler directed that the Army Group Centre's Panzer Group, led by Guderian, should move south-east on to Kiev. First Panzer Group also headed northward. This took away two of its most useful fighting units from the centre group.

Hitler had recognised that his most difficult decision was what to do after his forces had broken through the Stalin Line; whether to go north, south or continue east.

By November the German advance had stopped. They had not captured their principal targets; Leningrad, Moscow and Stalingrad, and the Soviet armed forces had not been defeated. Blitzkrieg did not work in the Soviet Union for various reasons:

Below is a list of reasons for Russia's survival in 1941:

- Timing. The invasion had been sanctioned only in June, which was too late in the year. There was not enough time for the German army to achieve its goals before winter.

- Too big. Operation Barbarossa was too much; with its three armies in three directions, it meant that the attack divided the German forces, which were meant to cover a territory that was roughly 500,000 square miles in size, with 75 million people to manage and control. The Germans also expected a short war, which would be over in the autumn and the German troops did not have winter clothing.

- Lack of preparation. Due to the war extending into the winter, the Germans ran into further problems that they were not prepared for. The 1941 Russian winter was very severe. German armoured vehicles could not operate in the sub-zero temperatures. The men did not even have winter clothing prepared, and many soldiers died of frostbite.

- Stalin provided firm authority and commanded the Soviet armies to withdraw so they could fight another day. During the Russian retreat, all supplies, anything the Germans could use, were destroyed. This is called a scorched earth policy.

- The weather was the most important reason. The weather conditions changed in November 1941 and created heavy rain, which destroyed the already weak Russian/Eastern European road system, which slowed the German armies.

- Russia had a vast population. The army losses could easily be replaced. The Germans expected the Russians to have 51 Divisions in reserve; they had 831 Divisions in reserve.

- Despite their significant advances, the Germans had lost too many men, tanks and fuel.

- Before the war, the Russians had set up many factories in the east to build more weapons. The factories were therefore out of German bomber range and could produce large amounts of materials for the war effort.
- Russia's road system was weak and slowed up German progress, and there was no plan in place to fix and maintain the rail systems.
- Russia was vast. She could afford to lose a lot of land and people and keep fighting.

The Americans arrive in Europe: The Battle of the Bulge.

Background:

This was a battle that was between the Americans, British and Germany. German General Von Mellenthin said: *"The Ardennes battle (The Battle of the Bulge) drives home the lesson that a large-scale offensive by massed armour has no hope of success against an enemy who enjoys supreme command of the air. Our precious reserves had been expended, and nothing was available to ward off the impending Catastrophe in the East."*

The two-month Battle of the Bulge (December 1944 – January 1945) was an aggressive German attack launched through the Ardennes region in Belgium, France, and Luxembourg on the Western Front, this time towards the end of the war. This surprise attack caught the Allied forces completely off guard. American forces endured the brunt of the assault and incurred their highest fatalities for any operation of the war. The battle also severely depleted Germany's armoured forces on the Western Front, which Germany was mostly unable to replace. German personnel and Luftwaffe aircraft also sustained heavy losses. The Battle of the Bulge was the most significant battle fought mainly by the Americans in Europe during World War Two. Over 600,000 American troops were involved in the fight.

The German plan:

- The 6th Panzer Army led by Sepp Dietrich was the main thrust of the attack, with the aim of capturing the city and port of Antwerp.
- The 5th Panzer Army was led by Manteuffel and was to attack the centre of the American forces, gain the critical road and rail centre of St Vith, and then drive on to Brussels.
- The 7th Army was to attack in the south and to create a buffer zone to stop American reinforcements from attacking the Fifth Panzer Army.
- The 15th Army was to be held back to counter any Allied attack which might take place.
- The battle started with a two-hour bombardment of the Allied lines, which was followed by a strong armoured attack with the bulk of the German armour based at the Schnee Eifel. The Germans achieved great success early on.

Events:

The Allies were taken by surprise; they had received little intelligence that such an attack would take place.

Before the attack started, English-speaking German soldiers disguised themselves in American uniforms, went behind Allied lines, and caused chaos by spreading misinformation, changing road signs and cutting telephone lines. Those German soldiers who were caught were shot after a court-martial.

The weather was also in the Germans' favour. A thick fog meant that the superior air force of the Allies could not be employed. Most importantly, the Allies could not use the tank-busting Typhoons of the RAF or the Mustang fighters of the USAAF. The weather was typical of the Ardennes in winter; it was foggy, and the ground was hard enough for army vehicles to cross. This suited the German tank assault.

However, the success of the Germans continued for just two days. Despite penetrating a bulge into the Allied front line, the Germans could not exploit this. They had based their plan of attack on a massive armoured onslaught. Nevertheless, they did not have enough fuel to maintain such an attack.

On December 22nd, the fog started to clear, allowing the Allies to bring their air power into action. On the following day, the Americans launched a counter-attack on the Germans.

On Christmas Eve, the Allies encountered the first attack by jet bombers. Sixteen German Me-262's attacked rail yards to affect the Allies' supply lines. However, without fuel for the ground attack, the armoured vehicles, any success in the air was meaningless.

The Germans had driven forward 60 miles in just two days, but from December 18th on, they were in a position of deadlock. The fighting was savage. The time around New Year's was a time of unusually intense fighting. The Germans started a second front in Holland. This coincided with a period of intense cold and rain, and the soldiers on the ground faced challenging conditions. For example, trench foot was a common problem for infantrymen, as was exposure.

By mid-January 1945, the lack of fuel was becoming evident as the Germans had to abandon their vehicles. The 1st SS Panzer Division had to make their way back to Germany on foot.

In total, the Americans lost 81,000 men while the Germans lost 100,000. They were either killed, wounded or captured.

Reasons for German loss.

A lack of fuel. Any form of armoured attack needs a constant supply of fuel, which they did not have. The allied bombing of fuel plants in Germany meant that this supply did not exist. They had limited to no air cover, and the jet fighters were not being made in large enough numbers.

Field Marshall von Rundstedt believed that *"all, absolutely all, conditions for the possible success needed for such an offensive were lacking."*

General von Mellenthin said: *"The Ardennes battle drives home the lesson that a large-scale offensive by massed armour has no hope of success against an enemy who enjoys supreme command of the air. Our precious reserves had been expended, and nothing was available to ward off the impending catastrophe in the east."*

Development of tank tactics by strategists: Guderian, Liddell Hart, Fuller.

Background:

This section looks at how developments in technology brought change to how future battles was to be waged on the land, sea and air. This is shown by the military theorists such as Guderian, Hart and Fuller.

Sir Basil Henry Liddell Hart

Sir Liddel Hart had served in the First World War as a soldier for the British and retired from the army in 1927. He began work as a journalist and developed some pieces on military strategy, based in part on his experiences in the First World War and further research. He wrote on mechanised warfare and suggested the infantry be carried along with the armoured and mechanized units. This was, therefore, a written piece on combining forces of infantry and armour, but the infantry follows in their own vehicles. This strategy and the inclusion of a strong air force was to have a significant effect on the political scene and was taken on board by then Prime Minister Chamberlain in 1937.

Major General John Frederick Charles Fuller

Shimon Naveh, former head of the Israel Defence Forces' Operational Theory Research Institute *"by manipulation and contrivance, Liddell Hart distorted the actual circumstances of the Blitzkrieg formation and obscured its origins. Through his indoctrinated idealization of an ostentatious concept, he reinforced the myth of Blitzkrieg. By imposing, retrospectively, his own perceptions of mobile warfare upon the shallow concept of Blitzkrieg, he created a theoretical imbroglio that has taken 40 years to unravel"*.

After WW2, Hart felt that the Wehrmacht had adopted ideas from Fuller.

General Fuller also served in the British army and wrote several military books. He also wrote about the nine principles of warfare in 1925. General Fuller's ideas of a tank army, which put heavy emphasis on massed armoured formations.

The Nine Principles:

1. Direction: What is the overall aim also known as a strategy? Which objectives must be met to achieve the aim?
2. Concentration: Where will the commander centre his most significant or most essential forces?
3. Distribution: Where and how will the commander place his forces?
4. Determination: The will to fight, the will to persist, and win must be continued.
5. Surprise.
6. Endurance: Your army's ability to handle pressure.
7. Mobility: The commander's ability to move their force while outmanoeuvring the enemy's army.

8. Offensive Action: The ability to gain and maintain the initiative in combat, which should disorganise the enemy.
9. Security: The ability to protect yourself from attack.

Heinz Guderian

Guderian was a German general who was one of the best Generals of WW2. In 1935 Guderian was given command of a Panzer Division. In 1937 he wrote the book, Achtung Panzer. Achtung Panzer is considered by some military historians to be a brilliant book, but still an evolution of thoughts that relied on previous theorists. Gudarian argues for the use of tanks and motorized support vehicles in mobile warfare, later known as Blitzkrieg tactics. The reason we can see this as evolution is that this had been witnessed in WW1, and during other conflicts we have studied, the Spanish Civil War and the Soviet Japanese war. The book also argues against using cavalry due to the effectiveness of the machine gun and suggests that cavalry with mechanised infantry. After the failure of Barbarossa, Adolf Hitler sacked Guderian.

Chapter 5:

The changing nature of air warfare

***

This chapter will be looking at:

- The Battle of Britain,
- The Blitz,
- V weapons
- The allied bombing of Germany.

Air warfare experienced swift changes during and after World War Two and became far more critical in deciding the outcome of conflicts.

During the Second World War:

Airpower played an essential role in:

Blitzkrieg used the Luftwaffe to target enemy aircraft and airfields; this would ensure that the Germans had control of the air. This was seen during the invasions of Poland, Belgium, Holland and France. Dive bombers and Stukas were used to support ground forces with the aim of creating maximum terror.

Dunkirk:

This was when the Royal Airforce (RAF) protected Allied troops on the beach, whilst they were waiting for evacuation from British vessels sent across the Channel to evacuate the Allied forces.

Battle of Britain

Background:

This was a battle between 卐 Germany and 🇬🇧 Britain.

"Never was so much owed by so many to so few" Winston Churchill

After the collapse of the Low Countries at the beginning months of World War 2, Hitler hoped that the British would surrender. They refused. Hitler began to look at other methods of getting the British to quit and concluded that an invasion would be necessary. Due to the British having superiority at sea, the German air force, the Luftwaffe, would need superiority in the air. This would then allow the seas to be cleared and then allow for a German amphibious landing. The codename for the planned German invasion of Britain was Operation Sea Lion.

The Battle of Britain was a series of fights taking place during the summer of 1940, almost daily. Waves of Luftwaffe bombers escorted by fighters attacked important targets, mainly in south-east England, and were often intercepted by British fighter planes.

British had 1000 fighters, 700 operational, 1380 pilots. Well organised defence system, which included spotters and Radar (**Ra**dio **d**etection **a**nd **r**anging.)

Germany had 1000 fighters, 800 operational, 870 pilots. Limited bomber experience due to the easy success of gaining air superiority and designed to support the army, not to create strategic victories.

Events:

On the 13 August, the Germans began full-scale raids on the South-East of England targeting radar and sector stations.

Five days later the Luftwaffe targeted airfields in Southern Britain trying to destroy the British fighter planes.

By early September, Britain had few fighter planes, working airfields and pilots left and was therefore close to defeat. However, on the 7th of September, Britain was lucky in some respects. On the verge of this air victory, Hitler gave Britain much needed time for its air force to recover by diverting the Luftwaffe to the bombing of London.

On the 15th of September, the Luftwaffe attempted to bomb London during daylight and lost 56 planes. Two days later Hitler decided to delay the invasion of Britain.

The RAF success:

Radar. Part of the reason for British success was that Britain had developed radar in the 1930s and by 1940 they had established a network of radar stations. They could detect the location of German aircraft, which would allow British fighter planes to get into position, in equal or superior numbers, and ready to attack. Due to the radar system, the Luftwaffe was generally unable to catch the British fighters on the ground and destroy them as they had with the Polish air force.

Communication. Britain also had a series of communication centres, section stations, which collected information from radar stations.

The British planes, Hurricanes and Spitfires, were equal to the German Messerschmitt 109.

The RAF pilots who bailed out over Britain could return to the fight, but German pilots became prisoners of war. This totalled just over 1000 prisoners of war.

German failures:

The Stuka was a dive bomber. It was designed to support ground forces but was not equipped to deal with enemy fighter planes.

The distance. German fighter planes had to fly from France and then over the channel before they could attack the British. This meant that they only had enough fuel for 30 minutes of flying. This meant that German bombers often flew without fighter planes to support them, making them easy targets for the British fighters. The Battle of Britain was vital because it prevented a German invasion, ensured British survival and provided a much-needed morale booster for the British public.

The British won because:

1. They had plenty of factories making new planes to replace those shot down.

2. German fighters protecting their bombers had a short range and had to break off combat before their fuel ran out, leaving the bombers vulnerable.

3. The British radar located German attacks and allowed the RAF to get ready to meet them.

4. British pilots who were shot down over Britain and survived could be sent back into action. Germans were taken prisoner because they were fighting over enemy territory.

5. The decision by the Germans to switch to bombing British cities meant the RAF kept control of the air and could stop an invasion by sea.

6. German losses in planes and crew were significant and harder to replace.

V for Vengeance, V weapons, the first cruise missiles.

In May 1941, Hitler called off the bombing campaign. He decided that the best way to achieve victory over the British was to defeat the Russians and therefore needed Luftwaffe to support the impending invasion of the Soviet Union.

Between 1944-45 the British experienced a second blitz from the V-1 and V-2 missiles.

Fired from Nazi-occupied Europe, V-1 flying bombs and V-2 supersonic missiles poured down on the south of England killing approximately 9,000 people. These 'Vengeance Weapons' were seen by Hitler as a way of winning World War Two and are viewed as the ancestors to today's missile technology.

V1

The V-1 was developed at Peenemünde Army Research Center by the Nazi German Luftwaffe during the Second World War. The first of the so-called Vergeltungswaffens designed for terror bombing of London, the V-1 was launched from facilities along the French and Dutch shores.

The first V-1 was fired at London on 13 June 1944), one week after (and prompted by) the successful Allied D-Day landings in Northern France. At its height, more than one hundred V-1s were fired a day at southeast England, 9,521 in total, diminishing in number as sites were overwhelmed until October 1944, when the final V-1 position in the range of Britain was captured by Allied forces.

After this, the V-1s were directed at the port of Antwerp and other targets in Belgium, with 2,448 V-1s being launched. The attacks stopped when the last launch site was overrun on 29 March 1945.

Unlike the V-2, the V-1 was a cost-effective weapon for the Germans as it forced the Allies to spend heavily on defensive measures and divert bombers from other targets. More than 25% of Combined Bomber Offensive's bombs in July and August 1944 were used against V-weapon sites, often ineffectively.

The cost to Germany	Blitz	V1	Allied air effort
Sorties	90,000	8,025	Sorties 86,800
Weight of bombs tons	61,149	14,600	Aircraft lost 1,260 351
Fuel consumed tons	71,700	4,681	Personnel lost 2,233 805
Aircraft lost	7,690	0	
Personnel lost	3,075	0	
Results	**Blitz**	**V1**	
Structures damaged/destroyed	1,150,000	1,127,000	
Casualties	92,566	22,892	
Rate casualties/bombs tons	1.6	1.6	

V-2 supersonic missiles

The V-2 was larger, faster and therefore more dangerous. With speeds of 4,000 kilometres an hour it was too fast to be shot down, and if you had the misfortune of it dropping near to you, it is more likely you would hear it before you saw it. It was a genuine guided missile (guided through mathematics) and flew at speeds of 4,000 kilometres an hour, this speed is known as supersonic. An estimated 500 V-2s hit London between September 1944 and March 1945, causing approximately 900 casualties. The missiles were developed too late in the war to have a decisive impact, and some historians have suggested that the work and resources could have been better used in other areas of war production.

The Blitz

The Blitz was Nazi Germany's continued aerial bombing campaign on Britain in World War Two. The bombing campaign killed an estimated 43,000 civilians and lasted for eight months, slowly reducing because Hitler began to focus on his plans for the Russian attack in May 1941.

The Blitz is a German word for 'lightning' and was applied by the British press due to the storm of heavy and regular bombing raids carried out over Britain in 1940 and 1941. This intensive, direct bombing of industrial objectives and civilian centres started in London on the 7th of September 1940 during what became known as the Battle of Britain. Hitler and Hermann Goering's plans to destroy the Royal Air Force ahead of an invasion of Britain were disappointing and, in response to an RAF raid on Berlin, they changed their tactics to the sustained bombing of civilian targets.

'Softening up' the British

The scale of the attack quickly escalated. In September, the Luftwaffe dropped an estimated 5,300 tonnes of high explosives on London in just 24 nights. Their aim was to 'soften up' the British by destroying morale before the planned invasion. Later, the German planes extended their targets to include the main coastal ports and centres of production and supply.

Taking cover

The British population had been warned by the British Government in September 1939 that air attacks on cities were likely and Government defence preparations had been started sometime before the announcement, both on a national and a local level. Those with gardens built simple corrugated steel Anderson shelters, covered over by soil. Larger civic shelters constructed of brick and concrete were raised in British towns, and a blackout was rigorously imposed after darkness.

The night raids became so common that they were nearly continuous. Many people who were tired of frequently hindering their sleep to go back and forth to the street shelters practically made them home. This created a new spirit of unity and community.

Londoners took what appeared to them an evident and sensible answer to the predicament and moved into the Tube stations in their thousands. At first, this was discouraged by the government. However, this popular action continued to the point that it had become a common sight for a commuter on the Underground to pass through a station crowded with the sleeping citizens with their belongings.

Sandwiched between the 7th of September 1940 and 21st of May 1941 there were significant air raids (Air raids are attacks by aeroplanes where more than 100 tons of high explosives were dropped) on 16 British cities. Over 267 days and nights, London was bombed 71 times, Birmingham, Liverpool and Plymouth eight times, Bristol six, Glasgow five, Southampton four, Portsmouth and Hull three, and there was also at least one massive raid on another eight cities.

A brief respite

The primary air offensive against British cities diminished after May 1941, with the change of direction of the German war machine towards Russia. However, sporadic and lethal raids, using increasingly bigger bombs, continued for several more years. In 1942, the 'Baedeker' raids targeted many the cities including Canterbury, York and Exeter, and the V1 and supersonic V2 rockets deployed between 1944 and 1945 killed nearly 9,000 civilians.

London

The primary target was the East end of London; this was due to the East End being full of factories and containing the docks. However, most of inner London suffered and the results of this can still be seen today, with areas of London still looking like the 1800s and other areas looking more modern. In total, 15,000 were killed and 250,000 made homeless. From the 2nd September to the 2nd November 1940 London was bombed every night. Key buildings like the House of Commons and Buckingham Palace were hit. The raids continued until early May 1941.

Coventry

The bombing of Coventry on 14 November 1940 caused an even more terrifying twist to the campaign. Five hundred German bombers released 500 tonnes of high bombs as well as nearly 900 incendiary bombs in ten hours.

Plymouth

In early 1941, the historic dockyards at Devonport were the primary target. The city was reduced to rubble in 5 raids with the final attack being on the 30th of April 1944. During the attacks, 1,172 civilians were killed and 4,448 injured.

Liverpool

From the 2nd of September to 2nd of November 1940, Liverpool was heavily bombed, causing nearly 4,000 deaths within the Merseyside area during the war. This city suffered its worst attack on the 3rd of May 1941. 500 bombers destroyed some of the most beautiful buildings and fires burned out of control for several days.

Belfast

Belfast was severely bombed in April and May 1940. At least 1,000 people were killed and 150,000 made homeless.

Glasgow

This city was bombed on the 13-14 March 1941 with the primary target being the shipyards on the Clyde. Over two nights over 500 people were killed, and hundreds wounded. Out of 12,000 houses, only seven were left undamaged.

The allied bombing of Germany.

The Allied bombing of Germany was one of the most controversial aspects of the Second World War. The attacks were carried out for several reasons:

- To disrupt German industrial production by targeting German industrial output and infrastructures.

- To reduce German morale.

In 1942, Air Marshall Harris became Head of British Bomber Command. He believed the Germans could be bombed into submission and that air power could be enough to defeat the Germans.

Overall, the Allied bombing only slightly reduced German war production but did prevent it from significantly expanding, arguably a 10% reduction. It also caused German aircraft to leave the Russian front, and it did affect the moral and everyday life of the German people.

Cologne:

In May 1942, the Allies started the first 'thousand bomber raid' on Cologne. It killed about 40,000 people.

Hamburg:

In 1943, Hamburg was virtually destroyed by a firestorm, which caused over 60,000 deaths and destroyed most of the city.

Berlin:

Due to Berlin being the capital of the Nazi Reich it was a regular target. June 7th, 1940 was the first bombing of Berlin. In total, roughly 68,000 tons of bombs were dropped. The largest bombing raid took place in February 1945, involving almost 1,600 aircraft and created a fire that lasted 4 days. The total number of who had died is estimated at 20 – 50,000 and roughly 16 km^2 had been turned to rubble.

Dresden:

In February 1945 Dresden was bombed. It was not an industrial centre and, moreover, the city was full of refugees fleeing the Russian front. Here, the Allies used incendiary bombs which then created a firestorm. A firestorm is a fire that is so large it can suck the oxygen out of the surrounding area, suffocating anyone in the area surrounding the firestorm. Estimates suggest that there were over 100,000 casualties in Dresden.

Criticism:

- Civilian casualties. There have been many criticisms of the Allied bombing especially with the use of incendiary bombs. It was morally wrong to target members of the public in cities such as Dresden as they had no military importance. The stories that came from people who experienced the bombing were shocking, to say the least. However, listening to veterans from the war, it has been suggested that we were not there and therefore have little knowledge or understanding of what was going through their minds when making decisions like the bombing of Dresden.

- It was counter-productive. Instead of reducing the morale of the German people, it made them even more determined to support the German policy of total war. Goebbels made practical use of the bombing for propaganda purposes, convincing many Germans that the Allies were evil.

- It had little effect on German industry. For example, it has been predicted that in 1944 German industrial output only fell by 10%. Most German industries adapted and moved underground.

- The cost of Allied lives, 140,000 airmen, and planes, 21,000, was too high considering the limited amount of damage. To many, it showed that bombing alone could not bring about the defeat of a resolute enemy. It was the progress of Allied troops from the West and Russian forces from the East which eventually brought about the German surrender.

Can you think of any exceptions that we have looked at so far, where bombing caused a country to quit fighting?

Summary of changes and continuity:

Changes:

Cruise missiles

V1/V2 missiles existed during World War 2, but no computer guidance system, mathematics, radio control and gyroscope allowed it to hit its target. Cruise Missiles, tomahawk missiles used in Gulf War 1 and 2, have computers installed, cameras, GPS and can target with the use of lasers.

Pilots

Pilots in the aircraft to remote-controlled aircraft

Example: WW2 aeroplanes required pilots

Take off

Traditional take off to vertical take-off.

Example: Vertical take-off experiments had existed in Nazi Germany but were prototypes and were not used in combat. This has changed with the Harrier jump jet, and Sea Harrier, which was used in the Falklands Conflict.

Propeller to a Jet engine.

Most planes used a propeller engine to fly into combat. Towards the end of the war, both the British and the Germans had developed Jet Engines, Britain's jets stayed inside the UK, and the first use of Jets was at the Battle of the Bulge. This has changed, and jet engine fighter aircraft have become the norm.

Continuity:

Drones have existed since WW1, yet their range and ability were severally limited by the ability to see the drone and to control the drone via radio controls, as well as only being used for surveillance. Drones today are still used for this purpose as well as now having the ability to be used in combat, such as in the first and second Gulf War.

V1/V2 was a prototype of a cruise missile.

Albeit the technology has changed, the principals of the missile have remained the same; a target is located, and the missile is fired at the said target, all without the requirement of a pilot.

Still required in the blitzkrieg, and deep battle.

Air support and air cover are crucial in modern day missions. The fundamental part of blitzkrieg led the initial attack, softened up the enemy, and once air superiority was established, victory was ensured. The Battle of the Bulge and invasion of Low Countries and France are clear examples of the effectiveness of aircraft support and air cover. These tactics are still used today with evidence in the Falklands, First and Second Gulf War.

Chapter 6:

Middle Eastern Conflict

***

This section will look at the importance of aircraft in Arab-Israeli Wars:
- The Six Day War
- The War of Yom Kippur
- First Gulf War
- The Second Gulf War

The Six Day War, 1967

Background:

This was a battle between Egypt and Syria against Israel that took place in the Middle East. Israel was country created due in part to the horrors suffered by the Jewish populations of Europe. The British gave territories in the Middle East, which created Israel. This has led to a series of conflicts and tensions in the Middle East between Israel and her new neighbours.

The President of Egypt, Gamal Abdel Nasser said: *"We shall not enter Palestine with its soil covered in sand, we shall enter it with its soil saturated in blood."*

According to President Attassi of Syria: *"...it is the duty of all of us now to move from defensive positions to offensive positions and enter the battle to liberate the usurped land...Everyone must face the test and enter the battle to the end."*

Prime Minister Levi Eshkol gave a speech that included the following: *"Given the fourteen incidents of sabotage and infiltration perpetrated in the past month alone, Israel may have no other choice but to adopt suitable countermeasures against the focal points of sabotage. Israel will continue to take action to prevent any and all attempts to perpetrate sabotage within her territory. There will be no immunity for any state which aids or abets such acts."*

Causes of the Conflict

While all sides agree that the first blow was struck by Israel, opinion differs on why the war started. This reflects the teaching of Western History to our GCSE students; there is always more than one side of an argument. Here there are three perspectives/interpretations of the cause of the war.

Think while reading: Which interpretation do you agree with?

1. Israel was behaving defensively. This was a pre-emptive strike against Arab nations who were likely to attack soon. Throughout the conflict, Israel acted with admirable restraint.

2. Israel was behaving aggressively. She purposely misunderstood the situation to justify starting a war of conquest and directed her attack mercilessly.

3. The war was the result of misinterpretations on both sides. The Arabs made aggressive comments against Israel, which made the Israelis believe the Arabs were planning to invade, but there was no real plot to invade Israel. However, Israel failed to realise this, so both sides ended up in a war they did not want.

Events:

In 1967, Israel launched an attack upon her Arab neighbours, claiming that they were about to attack her. The outcome was an Israeli victory.

Air power was to prove crucial. Israel's first and most important move was a surprise attack on the Egyptian Air Force. Egypt had the largest and the most modern of all the Arab air forces, consisting of about 420 combat aircraft, all of them Soviet-built. Attacks started that afternoon against Jordanian, Syrian, and Iraqi airfields, which wiped out most of those nations' air forces. By the nightfall of the first day, the Jordanian air force was obliterated. Afterwards, the air attacks the Israeli blitzkrieg tanks, supported by air attack, were carried out without fear of enemy attacks from the air.

Between the 10th to the 15th of June, the Israelis had won using the Blitzkrieg tactics of the Second World War, with more modern tanks and aircraft.

On the 5th of June, Israeli planes destroyed the Egyptian air force before it could get off the ground.

- Israeli tanks, supported by the air force, defeated Egyptian troops in the Sinai region.
- The Israeli air force destroyed the air power of Syria and Jordan and captured the Golan Heights, and with it the Syrian army.
- The Israeli army had the most modern planes and tanks, which were supplied by the USA.
- The use of speed and surprise.
- One unified command, capable of acting rapidly and decisively.
- They used tactics which ensured control of the air and the practical use of tank warfare, which was fitted the desert areas of the Sinai and Golan Heights.

Ever since this victory, the status of Gaza, the West Bank and Jerusalem have remained hotly disputed between Arabs and Israelis.

Which interpretation did you agree with the most?

The War of Yom Kippur, the October War 1973.

Background:

This was a battle between ▬ Israel and ▬ Egypt and ▬ Syria. During this conflict, the Arab states were successful at first but were later defeated by Israel. Part of their early success was due to the element of surprise.

(What tactic that we have looked at which uses the element of surprise?)

Events:

In October, on the Jewish Holy Day of Yom Kippur, Israeli forces were attacked by Egyptian and Syrian forces in the Sinai and on the Golan Heights. They inflicted heavy losses and damage on the Israelis.

The War of Yom Kippur, 1973, is the most recent 'full' war in the history of the Middle East. It is called this because it began on the Day of Atonement (Yom Kippur), the most sacred day of the Jewish calendar.

The war started with a surprise Arab attack on Israel on Saturday the 6th of October 1973. On this day, Egyptian and Syrian military forces launched an offensive, knowing that the Israeli military would be partaking in the Yom Kippur celebrations. Their guard, therefore, would temporarily be lowered.

Arab nations such as Egypt and Syria aided and financed the attack. Iraq transported Hunter jet fighter jets to Egypt a few months before the war began. Iraqi Russian-built MIG fighters fought against the Israelis in the Golan Heights, along with 18,000 Iraqi soldiers. Saudi Arabia and Kuwait financed the Arabic side in the war. Approximately 3,000 Saudi troops also fought in the war. Libya gave Egypt French-built Mirage fighters and in the years 1971 to 1973, Libya contributed $1 billion towards the modernisation of the Egyptian army, which was used to acquire modern Russian weaponry. Other Arabic nations that helped included Tunisia, Sudan and Morocco. Jordan also sent two armoured forces and three artillery units to aid the Syrians, but their assistance was less enthusiastic, probably because King Hussein of Jordan had not been fully informed about the Egyptian and Syrian plans.

The Arab Allies included: Iraq, Saudi Arabia, Kuwait, Libya, Tunisia, Sudan, Morocco and Jordan.

Facing such an attack, the Israeli forces were overwhelmed. Within two days, the Egyptians had crossed the Suez Canal and moved up to 15 miles inland of the Sinai. Syrian forces also advanced 15 miles to the Golan Heights in northern Israel. By the end of October 7th, Israel was facing a dangerous military situation.

Nevertheless, on the 8th of October, Israeli forces were bolstered by called-up reserves and counter-attacked in the Sinai. They drove back the Egyptian army and crossed the Suez Canal. The Israelis used the Suez-Cairo road to drive towards Cairo (the capital of Egypt) and got to within 65 miles of it.

The Israelis encountered similar success in the Golan Heights, where the Syrian forces were pushed back, and Israel recaptured the lost land. The Israelis got to within 35 miles of the Syrian capital Damascus.

On the 24th of October, a cease-fire was established by the United Nations. The UN sent peacekeepers to the highly unstable regions affected by the combat. Between January and March, Israeli and Egyptian forces stopped fighting along the Suez Canal. Here, the Israelis controlled the strategic Sinai Desert. This area allowed Israel a buffer zone; an area that would ensure any fighting near the Suez Canal did not spill over into Israel itself.

In May 1974, 1200 United Nations troops were sent to keep the peace in the Golan Heights. They formed a buffer zone between Syria and Israel.

Dr Henry Kissenger, the then American Secretary of State (a person selected by the President of the United States to represent the United States abroad), acted as a peacemaker between Egypt and Israel. By September 1975, Egypt and Israel signed an agreement which stated their willingness to resolve their disputes and differences by peaceful means.

Some Arabs felt that Egyptian leader Anwar Sadat had betrayed their cause, and this cost him his life in 1981. In October 1973, Sadat had adopted an aggressive approach to Arab relations with Israel. He was a saviour to the Palestinians in Israel. His diplomatic approach to solving the region's problems was too much for some Arabs.

What did Israel get out of the Yom Kippur War?

Although there was the initial progress of the Egyptian and Syrian armies, the war demonstrated again how capable the Israeli military could be. After the initial setbacks, the conflict served as a huge morale booster to the Israelis. Despite a coordinated assault on two fronts, Israel had survived and had pushed back the nations that had initially broken through their defences.

The Americans sold the Israeli military weaponry and they also provided Israel with intelligence reports, which proved to be far more critical. Therefore, the Israelis knew where their enemy was and could coordinate an attack accordingly.

Documents relating to the SR-71 (an American spy-plane) show that the Israelis knew where to find significant concentrations of Arab forces. With this information, the Israelis knew where to deploy their troops for maximum effect. What appeared to be devastating and intuitive counter-attacks by the Israelis, were in fact based on this very detailed information. The war also served as a lesson to the Arab nations that surrounded Israel in that initial victories had to be built on.

How does this differ from the success of the Germans in WW2 in Poland and France?

Surprise and speed did little to help the Egyptian and Syrian forces; there was no strategy to get to an end, which would have been to push the Israelis back until you got to a conclusion. Instead, the Syrians stopped the advance and the Egyptians had to then go on a further offensive, which took them away from their aerial defences. This allowed the Israelis a chance to gather forces, and to defeat the Syrians. This then pushed

Sadat towards adopting a diplomatic approach. It also encouraged some Palestinians towards more extreme actions.

The First Gulf War: Operation Desert Shield

This was a change from Blitzkrieg to air - land battle/Deep battle.

Background:

This conflict that involved many nations, including Iraq, Kuwait, Saudi Arabia, the USA, Britain, and France. The Arab-Israeli Wars had continued to confirm the importance of controlling the air. The First Gulf War was the first military campaign where the ground forces supported the air offensive. However, it still highlighted the importance of land forces in defeating the enemy.

In August 1990, the dictator of Iraq, Saddam Hussein, invaded the oil-rich state of Kuwait, which was south of Iraq. Saddam did not think that the Americans would object to the invasion because he had been an ally of the USA, there were even rumours that this had been given the go-ahead by the US intelligence agencies. However, the USA and Britain, supported by other countries, forced Saddam out of Kuwait.

In 1990 Iraq accused Kuwait of stealing Iraqi petroleum through slant drilling, although some Iraqi sources indicated that Saddam Hussein's decision to attack Kuwait had been made a few months before the actual invasion.

There were numerous reasons for the Iraqi move, including Iraq's inability to pay more than US$80 billion that had been borrowed to bankroll the Iran–Iraq war, and Kuwaiti overproduction of petroleum, which kept revenues down for Iraq. The invasion started on 2 August 1990. Within two days the Kuwait Armed Forces were either overrun by the Iraqi Republican Guard or had fallen back to neighbouring Saudi Arabia and Bahrain. The Emirate of Kuwait was annexed, and Saddam Hussein announced a few days later that it was now the 19th province of Iraq.

Events:

The campaign was in two stages:
- ➢ Stage 1 was an air offensive, which was launched on the 16th of January 1991 and lasted for almost a month. In a short time, a variety of military air vehicles, including stealth aircraft, cruise missiles and precision-guided weapons, severely damaged Iraq's military and economic infrastructure.

> Stage 2 was the counter-invasion known as Operation Desert Saber. It was launched on the 23rd of February. Land forces advanced into Kuwait and had liberated the country within four days.

The Invasion of Kuwait, also known as the Iraq–Kuwait War, was a significant conflict between Iraq and Kuwait. This was caused by the seven-month-long Iraqi control of Kuwait and afterwards led to the direct military invasion by US-led forces in the Gulf War, and the setting alight by Iraq of 600 Kuwaiti oil wells.

The Air war began on 17 Jan 1991. The air attacks had four main target areas: Command and Control, Air Superiority, destruction of Weapons of Mass Destruction (WMD), and the Republican Guard. The plan was to carry out a strategic bombing, whilst gaining air superiority, to bomb the Iraqi artillery, troops and trenches, and then finally launch a ground offensive against a severely weakened opponent.

Smart bombs were not very accurate. For example, the F-117 hit of 55% of its targets, while the older F-111 hit the target 70% of the time with laser-guided bombs. The most important part was the ground assault. Only ground forces, in particular infantry. This has shown time and time again that the only way to take and hold ground was with infantry. Although airpower was vital in softening up the Iraqi trenches and troops, it is nearly impossible to dislodge or destroy an opposing army without the use of ground troops. (So: has anything changed in warfare?)

Air Superiority was soon won, 116 Iraqi aircraft fled to Iran where they were seized. To have complete control over the air is very rare in warfare, and it allowed the usually vulnerable helicopter Gunships to roam at will across the open battleground.

Battle on Land

The Iraqi invasion of Saudi Arabia (Battle of Khafji), the Hammer and the Anvil.

On 29 January, Iraqi forces attacked and occupied the lightly defended Saudi city of Khafji with tanks and infantry. The Battle of Khafji ended two days later when the Iraqis were driven back by the Saudi Arabian National Guard, supported by Qatari forces and U.S. Marines. The allied forces used artillery fire.

This is called an Air-Land battle (also known as Deep Battle). It is a change. Because of modern weapons with extended range, an attack does not just strike the enemy front lines but rather the whole military organisation. It attacks the front, artillery, reserves and most importantly the command and control centre (C&C). Without this, the troops are potentially blind and helpless.

The ground assault began on 24th Feb 1991 and lasted precisely 100 hours; the speed was intense. The plan was a general attack along a broad front with false attacks in the south, near Kuwait, and the left flank (The North) swinging around like a huge left hook or hammer.

2 US armoured divisions were to push north, then east, and pin the Republican Guard against the sea and destroy them. If it went south, the British forces were to form a block, also known as the anvil, and the 2 US divisions would swing back towards the British like a hammer.

1. The **first day** went well. The Iraqis, who were expected to fight stubbornly, were steamrolled by the Coalition forces, with no recon, inadequate supplies and their armour being wholly outclassed. Progress was rapid. Coalition casualties on the first day were eight dead and twenty-seven wounded.

2. On the **second day,** sandstorms stopped most air resupply missions. However, thanks to satellites, also known as GPS, the Coalition forces were still able to advance slowly, frequently taking Iraqi units by surprise in the poor weather conditions.

3. On the **third day**, clouds limited aerial reconnaissance, but the advance continued. It became a race to catch and destroy the Republican Guard before they escaped to Iraq. As dawn began, the British forces attacked a large enemy position with a two-pronged armoured attack and one division, attacking them from the rear and clearing out the prepare position.

Air warfare

The Gulf War began with an extensive aerial bombing campaign on the 17th of January. The Coalition flew over 100,000 sorties, which dropped 88,500 tons of bombs, and causing widespread destruction to military and civilian infrastructure.

The next Coalition targets were command and communication facilities. Saddam Hussein had closely micromanaged Iraqi forces in the Iran–Iraq War, and initiative at lower levels was discouraged. Coalition planners hoped that Iraqi resistance would quickly collapse if deprived of command and control.

The air campaign's third and most significant phase targeted military targets throughout Iraq and Kuwait: Scud missile launchers, weapons research facilities, and naval forces. About one-third of the Coalition's air power was devoted to attacking Scuds, some of which were on trucks and therefore difficult to locate. U.S. and British special operations forces had been secretly inserted into Iraq, to aid in the search for, and destruction of, Scuds.

Operation Desert Sabre, a massive allied ground offensive, was launched northward from north-eastern Saudi Arabia into Kuwait and southern Iraq on February 24. Within three days Arab and U.S. forces had retaken Kuwait City, and Iraqi opposition crumbled. Meanwhile, the chief U.S. armoured thrust drove into Iraq some 120 miles west of Kuwait and attacked Iraq's armoured reserves from the rear. By February 27, these units had destroyed most of Iraq's elite Republican Guard units. U.S. President George Bush declared a cease-fire for February 28, by which time Iraqi resistance had collapsed entirely.

There are no official numbers for the Iraqi military operation. Estimates of the number of Iraqi troops in the Kuwait theatre range from 180,000 to 630,000 and estimates of Iraqi military deaths range from 8,000 to 100,000. The allies, by contrast, lost about 300 troops in the conflict.

Essential ground forces started to move on 23 February. Aircraft had long been patrolling, attacking targets of opportunity, and bombing assigned targets, flying 900 sorties on the eve of the attack. Now, however, the beat of rotors joined the roar of jet engines as the 101st Airborne Division began flying helicopters into Western Iraq. 48 hours before the main assault, Coalition air forces concentrated on attacking the Iraqi forces.

It was considered politically essential that Arab forces free Kuwait City. Since the U.S. Marines had better engineering equipment and obstacle breaching techniques, they led the movement into Kuwait. As they moved through the first line of border defences, two Saudi armoured brigades and a pan-Arab brigade (the same Arab units which had retaken Khafji) entered Kuwait.

Helicopter-borne 1st Division Marines moved through the second break in the Iraqi defensive. The 2nd Division attacked, successfully, at a point that appeared so well fortified that the Marines decided the Iraqis were unlikely to actively defend it.

It was also becoming evident that the Iraqi forces in Kuwait, partially due to high rates of desertion, were considerably smaller than expected. B-52 attacks even aimed away from troops, terrified them and caused them to run away.

With the Iraqi evacuation and the successful movement of light forces in the west, the main attack started early. As it entered, the 101st's attack helicopters were already destroying Iraqi trucks on highways in the rear area. Before long, the Americans had penetrated at least fifteen miles. The Marines captured one headquarters and were taking so many Iraqi prisoners that they could only disarm them, point south, and tell them where to walk to Prisoner of War Camps (POW camps).

On the 24th, the Americans advanced to Kuwait City. In the first phase, they captured an entire Iraqi battalion, then fought for Al Jaber airfield and captured another 3000 men. By the end of the day, they had over 10,000 unexpected prisoners and were now 20 miles inside Kuwait.

After four days of battle, all Iraqi troops were expelled from Kuwait, ending a nearly seven-month invasion of Kuwait by Iraq. Over 1,100 casualties were suffered by the Coalition. Estimates of Iraqi casualties range from 30,000 to 150,000. Iraq lost thousands of vehicles, while the advancing Coalition lost relatively few; Iraq's old Soviet T-72 tanks were no match for the American M1 Abrams and British Challenger tanks.

Actions in the Gulf Sea

Around 20% of the sorties launched by U.S. air power came from the carriers in the Gulf and the Red Sea. The six carriers on the station were used to start a variety of raids against strategic and tactical targets, along with support and command operations for Navy and Marine aircraft in the theatre. Despite fears of anti-ship missile attack, the six carriers emerged from the battle unscathed.

The Second Gulf War, 2003

Background:

This was a battle that mainly involved Britain, the USA and Iraq. This began in March 2003. US forces were backed by Britain and other countries, invaded Iraq.

This was due to three key reasons:

- Alleged involvement in terrorism
- Alleged development of arms of mass destruction

73

- To free the people of Iraq from his dictatorship

Events:

On the 19th of March, U.S. Stealth bombers and Tomahawk Cruise Missiles struck targets in and around the Iraqi capital of Baghdad. This is a critical difference in Deep Battle to Blitzkrieg. The US military can affect the entire country simultaneously with air attacks. You cripple the whole of military infrastructure of a country, not just the areas immediately able to reinforce.

On the 20th of March, the U.S. and British troops and armoured divisions advanced into southern Iraq, entering the port city of Umm Qasr, near the major Iraqi city of Basra, while the second wave of air bombardments hit Baghdad.

On the 23rd of March, the Coalition forces captured airfields in western Iraq and controlled parts of Umm Qasr, Basra and Nasiriyah. The mechanised forces advanced to within 100 miles of Baghdad and forced a crossing of the Euphrates River at Nasiriyah, where Iraqi troops put up stiff resistance. In northern Iraq, the U.S. launched 40 to 50 cruise missiles on two Islamist parties opposed to the Pro-U.S. political parties.

On the 29th of March U.S. forces advanced as far north as Karbala, where massive battles with Iraqi forces took place. Air attacks on Baghdad and other Iraqi cities continued, as did Iraqi attempts to hit Kuwaiti-based targets with surface-to-surface missiles. One missile successfully hit Kuwait City on March 28, inflicting damage on a shopping mall and causing minor wounds to two Kuwaitis civilians.

On the 30th of March 600 British commandoes attacked near Basra, destroying Iraqi tanks and capturing roughly 300 prisoners.

On the 5th of April U.S. armoured forces entered Baghdad, conducting an extensive raid. This would continue for several days.

Finally, on the 7th of April, British forces reached the centre of Basra and declared that the city was under Coalition control.

The significance of the conflict

- No evidence was found that Saddam had been developing weapons of mass destruction.
- No evidence was found that linked Saddam to the 9/11 terrorist attacks.
- Saddam Hussein was overthrown and eventually captured by the Coalition.
- Coalition forces occupied Iraq to stabilise the economy and establish a democratic government. However, during their time, British and US troops faced various groups using urban and standard guerrilla tactics coupled with terrorist tactics.
- The Coalition victory was due to the successful deployment of conventional forces and traditional tactics of the second half of the twentieth century.

Chapter 7:

Guerrilla Warfare

***

This section will look at the importance of aircraft in Arab- Israeli Wars:
- Purpose of Guerrilla Warfare or Blitzkrieg
- Blitzkrieg vs guerrilla Strategy
- Strategy and tactics of Guerrilla Warfare
- Vietnam war
- Afghanistan war
- Civilian Resistance Movements: France & Yugoslavia

Che Guevara said:

"Why does the guerrilla fighter fight? We must come to the inevitable conclusion that the guerrilla fighter is a social reformer, that he takes up arms responding to the angry protest of the people against their oppressors, and that he fights to change the social system that keeps all his unarmed brothers in ignominy and misery"

Purpose of Guerrilla Warfare or Blitzkrieg

Force capitulation when combined with external political, economic and military pressures.

Or

Weaken to minimise his resistance against military blows that will follow.

Blitzkrieg vs guerrilla Strategy; Infiltration vs Isolation

Guerrilla warfare is a form of irregular war where a small group of combatants, such as armed civilians, use military tactics including ambushes, sabotage, raids, petty warfare, hit-and-run tactics, and mobility to fight a more substantial and less-mobile traditional military.

Blitzkrieg and guerrillas infiltrate a nation or regime at all levels to soften and shatter the morale of the political, economic and social structure of the country. Simultaneously, via diplomatic, psychological and other activities, they strip away potential allies. This then hopefully isolates the intended victim for further attacks. To carry out this program is like the methods seen and described by Sun Tzu, blitz and guerrillas:

Probe and test adversary, and any allies that may rally to his side, to unmask strengths, weaknesses, manoeuvres and intentions.

Exploit critical differences of opinion, internal contradictions, frictions, obsessions, etc., to incite mistrust, sow discord and shape both adversary's and allies' perception of the world thereby:

Create an atmosphere of 'mental confusion, the contradiction of feeling, indecisiveness, panic'…

Manipulate or undermine the adversary's military planning and actions

To make it difficult, if not impossible, for allies to aid their ally during their war and battles.

Strategy and tactics of guerrilla warfare.

The strategy and tactics of guerrilla warfare tend to concentrate on the use of a small, mobile force competing against a larger, more cumbersome one. The guerrilla focuses on organising in small units, depending on the assistance of the local population, as well as taking advantage of the local terrain.

Tactically, guerrilla armies avoid any confrontation with large units of enemy troops but seek and eliminate small groups of soldiers to minimise losses and weaken the opposing force. They also do not limit their targets. They will aim for enemy resources as a preferred target. All of that is to reduce the enemy's strength, to cause the enemy ultimately to be unable to continue fighting and therefore withdraw.

Guerrilla warfare can be replicated anywhere there is cover and where the advantages of cover cannot be used by a more significant and/or conventional force.

Leaders like Mao Zedong and North Vietnamese Leader Ho Chi Minh both used guerrilla warfare. Giving it a base, which served as a model for similar strategies elsewhere, such as Mujahideen in Afghanistan.

Mao Zedong summarised basic guerrilla tactics as:

"The enemy advances, we retreat; the enemy camps, we harass; the enemy tires, we attack; the enemy retreats, we pursue."

Communist leaders like Mao Zedong and North Vietnamese Ho Chi Minh both employed guerrilla warfare in the style of 'The Art of War.'

Guerrilla warfare tactics originated in the 20th century; it was considered to be irregular warfare. It has existed throughout the battles of many ancient civilisations, but smaller in scale. This was inspired in part by the theoretical works on guerrilla warfare, beginning with the Manual de Guerra de Guerrillas, Manual of war of Guerrillas, by Matías Ramón Mella, and more recently, Mao Zedong's, On Guerrilla Warfare, Che Guevara's Guerrilla Warfare and Lenin's text also called Guerrilla warfare. All were written after the successful revolutions carried out by them in China, Cuba and Russia respectively.

Those texts characterised the tactic of guerrilla warfare as according to Che Guevara's writing:

"used by the side which is supported by a majority, but which possesses a much smaller number of arms for use in defence against oppression".

The Vietnam War:

Background:

This was a war between the USA and North Vietnam; other countries were also involved. This war was over many different things, but the main point was the ideology. America, fearful of other countries becoming Communist, wanted to put a stop to it by using all its military might against the North Vietnamese, who were Communist.

Events:

The Vietcong was the name of the Communist guerrilla army who were partly from the south of Vietnam and from North Vietnam. They mainly used guerrilla tactics to fight because they could not match the strength of the US military, its resources and equipment. The North Vietnamese Army (NVA) and Vietcong were no match for the USA and the Army of the Republic of Vietnam (ARVN) in open warfare. The leader of the Communist was Ho Chi Minh. He had studied the guerrilla tactics used by China's communist leader Mao Zedong in the 1930s and 1940s. Mao had been successful in his struggle against the Capitalist Chinese Nationalist Party. Ho Chi Minh was also experienced in the use of these tactics because he had used them against the Japanese during the Second World War and the French in the years that followed.

These tactics were dependent on the support of the local peasantry, who would be expected to hide the Vietcong. The Vietcong fighters in return were supposed to be respectful to the villagers and, where possible, helpful. However, it is estimated that between 1966 and 1971, the Vietcong killed 27,000 civilians. They were prepared to kill peasants who opposed them or who co-operated with the capitalists/Americans. They used a variety of tactics including assassinations on police, tax collectors, teachers and other employees of the government of South Vietnam.

Theory of Guerrilla Warfare in Vietnam

This tactic aims to use small groups to attack the enemy by surprise, then disappear into the surrounding countryside.

Eventually, this would wear down the American forces and destroy their morale.

The Viet Cong were intelligent and skilful in the way they fought the Americans. They knew they could not match the American resources, so they used the jungle environment to their advantage. A vast network of underground tunnels, storage bases, workshops, kitchens, hospitals and barracks were built. The Vietcong could lay in wait and hide from the Americans. The Viet Cong used the jungle to their advantage and made it hard for the Americans to take on their enemy.

The Vietcong, a group of communist fighters in South Vietnam, used guerrilla tactics to achieve success. This meant that they launched surprise jungle attacks on the enemy. The Vietcong were almost impossible to identify. Since they had the assistance of most of the local population, they could quickly be assimilated back into village life and they were given aid to build underground tunnels to run away and hide from the Americans. They also dressed similarly to Vietnamese civilians and so it was hard for the Americans to identify their Vietcong enemy.

The tactics aimed to wear down and destroy an enemy soldier's morale. This was very effective, as soldiers were in continuous fear of ambushes and booby traps. In fact, 11% of American deaths were caused by booby traps. These were cheap, easy to make and useful. For example, sharpened bamboo stakes, hidden in shallow pits under sticks and leaves. The bamboo was so sharp that it could easily pierce a boot. Cheap, easy to make and hard to find.

They attacked and then retreated into the jungle, into the villages or their tunnels. The tunnels were booby-trapped, able to operate and exist without outside support and provided not only refuge from the bombing but also a haven for the guerrilla fighters. They were also generally a death trap for US and ARVN forces. Over 250 kilometres of tunnels were built in Vietnam, some of which passed under US military bases.

Weird fact: 250 kilometres is roughly the same circumference as the whole outer edge of London. Imagine digging a tunnel that long!

Reasons for Communist Victory:

Guerrilla tactics proved decisive because of several factors:

- Peasants in Vietnam had been alienated by different American policies, including Strategic Hamlets and Search and Destroy tactics. Many Vietcong were recruited from the local villages.
- Ho Chi Minh Trail was essential. Supplies from the North were coming to South Vietnam via a set of roads called the Ho Chi Minh Trail that ran through neighbouring Cambodia. There were up to 40,000 Vietnamese working to keep the trail open, and many of the supplies were provided by the Soviet Union and China.
- Knowledge and understanding of the jungles of South Vietnam. The US attempted to destroy the jungles using chemicals such as Agent Orange. However, this only alienated the local population.
- Inexperience. The USA had no experience or knowledge of guerrilla/jungle warfare carried out by the Vietcong. This inexperience was worsened by the fact that most of the US troops, especially after 1967, were not full combat troops but men (nineteen was the average age) who were conscripted into the armed forces and generally served only one year in Vietnam.

Afghanistan 1979

Background:

This was a war between the Soviet Union and Afghanistan. The Soviet-Afghan War lasted over 9 years from December 1979 to February 1989. Groups known as the Mujahideen received aid from several Western countries and several Muslim countries to help fight against the Soviet Army and allied Afghanistan armies. Between 850,000 to 1.5 million civilians were killed, and millions of Afghans fled the country as refugees, mostly to Pakistan and Iran.

The Mujahideen are Muslim rebels, who use guerrilla warfare against the invading Soviet forces. They believed fighting the Russians, they would go straight to paradise. They were supplied with sophisticated weaponry by the USA, Britain and China.

Events:

The Soviet forces

The USA felt that the Russians might be aiming for the Gulf [Middle East] region because of Oil. The Russian troops were poorly paid, lacked essential equipment and food and were beginning to have serious doubts about their government.

The invasion was broadcast around the World.

Guerrilla tactics were successful in Afghanistan in the 1980s. In December 1979, the Soviet Union invaded Afghanistan, setting up a puppet government that was supported by the Soviet army. This occupation faced opposition from Muslim fundamentalists known as the Mujahideen. These were mostly Afghan tribesmen trying to defeat one of the superpowers by using guerrilla tactics. The guerrillas focused on both civilian and military targets, knocking out bridges, shutting essential roads, attacking convoys, disrupting the electric power system, general industry, police stations, Soviet military bases, assassinating government officials and laying siege to small rural outposts.

The USSR wasted a fortune in trying to deal with the Mujahideen. Finally, in 1988, they withdrew from Afghanistan having suffered casualties of over 20,000 with most of the country in the control of the Mujahideen. Once again guerrilla tactics had been successful against an enemy with far more significant resources and human resources.

The Mujahideen were recruited from, and were generally supported by, the local population, many of whom hated the Russians and operated from roughly 4,000 bases.

The terrain was ideal, a mountainous area tailor-made for ambushes.

Pakistan provided much-needed supplies as well as training bases for the activities of the Afghan guerrillas.

Like the Vietnamese, they used hit-and-run tactics, attacking Soviet troops and supply lines and then disappearing into the local countryside. The Mujahideen favoured sabotage. The more common types of destruction involved attacking power lines, pipelines, radio stations, government buildings, air terminals, hotels, cinemas, and so on.

Reasons for Russian failure:

The Soviet Army of 1980 was trained and equipped for large-scale, conventional warfare in Europe against a similar opponent, i.e. it used armoured and motor-rifle formations. This was notably ineffective against small-scale guerrilla groups using hit-and-run tactics in the rough terrain of Afghanistan. The massive Red Army formations weren't mobile enough to engage small groups of Mujahideen fighters that smoothly meshed back into the territory. The strategy meant that troops were discouraged from 'tactical initiative', essential in countering guerrilla warfare because it could upset operational timing or command structure.

The Russians used large-scale attacks against Mujahideen strongholds, such as in the Panjshir Valley, which temporarily cleared the sectors and killed many civilians in addition to enemy combatants. The most significant failing was the fact that once the Russians did engage the enemy in force, they failed to hold the ground. Instead, they withdrew from the area once their operation was completed. If any civilians were killed, it could further alienate civilians from the Soviets, and this was to create dangerous effects later in the form of terrorist attacks such as 9/11.

The Soviets didn't have enough men, and their troops were not motivated. The peak number of Soviet soldiers was 115,000. Most of these troops were conscripts, which led to reduced combat performance.

Intelligence gathering, essential for success, was inadequate. The Soviets relied on aerial reconnaissance and radio intercepts rather than their reconnaissance infantry and their special forces. Although their special forces and reconnaissance infantry performed very well in combat against the Mujahideen, they would have better served in intelligence collection.

The Soviet media, for several years, hid the truth of how badly the war was going, which caused a backlash when the truth and its horrors were finally revealed.

However, the Russians did have elite infantry units, such as the Spetsnaz and their reconnaissance infantry. The problem with Spetsnaz and other specialised units was not their abilities, but that there were not enough of them and that they were employed incorrectly.

Summary of changes and continuity:

Changes:

Blitzkrieg to Deep Battle

Blitzkrieg only affected a small area of land, (especially when compared to deep battle) and had a battlefront; a line where the fighting took place. Poland and the Low Countries and France would be examples of this. They attacked what was in front of them and just behind where they were fighting.

Deep Battle, with the development of technology, allowed combatants to attack an entire country simultaneously. Gulf War One and Two allowed the allies to attack significant points of infrastructure, communications, electricity production and military installations across the country.

Blitzkrieg vs Guerrilla Warfare

Guerrilla warfare changed conflict in its aims. The aims were not to capture and hold territory, nor to kill the enemy, but to continuously harass the enemy until they quit, in the case of Vietnam or Afghanistan.

Continuity:

Blitzkrieg to Deep Battle

The principals are still the same. Use aerial combat to soften up the enemy, attacking points that would be crucial to continuing the war effort, then to send in tanks and infantry. The tanks and infantry would aim to break through weak points, and then move past strong points, eventually leaving the strong points surrounded and isolated.

Blitzkrieg vs Guerrilla Warfare

Blitzkrieg and Guerrilla warfare both use the element of surprise, Dein Bein Phu, and Operation Barbarossa, and attack enemy weak points or at their most vulnerable spot to achieve victory. To avoid strong points is also crucial. Vietcong and the Nazis both aimed to punch through a hit and run tactic of never stopping in the movement; they would both attack and move past the enemy to the next goal.

Civilian resistance movements:

France under German occupation.

Background:

This was a conflict between French civilians and Germany. In France: After the fall of France at the beginning of World War 2, French civilians independently and throughout France decided to work against the German occupying civilians.

General Charles de Gaulle, BBC radio broadcast (18th June 1940)

I, General de Gaulle, now in London, call on all French officers and men who are at present on British soil, or may be in the future, with or without their arms; I call on all engineers and skilled workmen from the armaments factories who are at present on British soil, or maybe in the future, to get in touch with me. Whatever happens, the flame of the French resistance must not and shall not die.

Dwight D. Eisenhower, Crusade in Europe (1948)

Throughout France, the Resistance had been of inestimable value in the campaign. Without their great assistance, the liberation of France would have consumed a much longer time and meant greater losses to ourselves.

Methods of Resistance included sabotage, assistance to the Allies, active and passive resistance.

Events:

Sabotage:

There were scattered acts of sabotage, but they were disorganized and, in most cases, quickly arrested by the authorities. Different groups became involved in the movement, including independent groups, school children, members of academia, the communist party, socialist party and members of the government.

The main objectives were:

(1) Execution of traitors and agents of the Gestapo

(2) Cutting of rail lines, with the derailment of enemy trains

(3) Destroying enemy telegraphic installations

(4) Cutting off logistics from factories production to stop or limit production

(5) Industrial sabotage of priority factories

In occupied France, the Gestapo began hunting members of the Communist Party and Socialist Party. Most went into hiding into the forests of the unoccupied zones. The Germans had only taken control of the Northern parts of France; the south was controlled by a French puppet government known as the Vichy Government. Soldiers from the defeated French Army also fled to these areas. These men and women formed themselves into units based on politics and geography. Eventually, they formed a group called 'the Maquis'. As the organization grew in strength, it began to attack Germans, as well as helping allied pilots downed over France get back to Britain.

Before the D-Day landings, instructions were sent to the French resistance, to attack German occupying forces. This included attacks on German garrisons in the towns of Tulle and Gueret. This also included armed resistance groups slowing down the 2nd SS Panzer Division from getting to the Normandy beaches.

General Dwight D. Eisenhower stated:

"Throughout France, the Resistance had been of inestimable value in the campaign. Without their great assistance, the liberation of France would have consumed a much longer time and meant greater losses to ourselves."

Passive Resistance:

One of the first public shows of resistance to the German occupation was on the 11th of November 1940 when school children came out on to the streets of Paris and marched to the Arc de Triumph, which celebrated the Allied victory over Germany in World War One.

A group of scientists and lawyers in Paris led by Boris Vilde began publishing the newspaper Musée de L'Homme calling on the French people to resist the German occupation. The Musée de L'Homme group was eventually infiltrated by a supporter of the Vichy government. Finally, almost all the men and women involved were arrested and executed.

General Charles De Gaulle persuaded the eight major resistance groups to form the Conseil National de la Resistance (CNR), and the first meeting took place in Paris on 27th May 1943.

In April 1943, the German Army began a campaign of repression throughout France. This included a policy of punishments against civilians living in towns and villages close to anywhere German soldiers had been attacked by members of the French Resistance.

Yugoslavia. Civilian Resistance of World War 2:

This was a conflict between Yugoslavia resistance groups and Nazi Germany.

Background:

Yugoslavia was a relatively new country and had been created because of World War One, by the Allies in recognition of their efforts in defeating Germany. On April 6th, 1941, the Germans invaded Yugoslavia and within 10 days the country surrendered.

There were two resistance Groups against the Germans, Tito's Communist Partisans and Colonel Mihailovich's Chetniks (Chetniks').

Chetniks

The first resistance to the Germans was the Chetniks led by Colonel Mihailovich; they were initially Serbian Special Forces trained to operate in occupied territory. Mihailovich was unique in guerrilla warfare, as he had advocated the war style before the outbreak of World War Two, and the Balkan wars. This was one of the first guerrilla resistance groups in Europe, and they were supported by the British Government. Serbians loyal to the Serbian government in exile took to the hills 100 miles from the city of Belgrade. It was ideal Guerrilla warfare territory. The Chetniks were mainly led by officers. Their first decisions included declaring themselves as a resistance movement, to recruit from Serbia and the Chetnik organisation, and once they had grown, they would begin to attack, disrupt and sabotage. Their tactics included attacking German arms depots, spreading false information and capturing towns occupied by the Germans. In 1941, the Chetniks began a liberation process and began to liberate the first towns of World War Two, including the towns of Cacak and Loznica. By the end of 1941, 5 towns had been liberated and a postal service had been established! However, the German response was that for every German killed they would kill 100 Serbs; for a wounded German, 50 Serbs would be killed.

Operation Mihailovich

The operation was an attempt to capture the Chetniks and Partisans by German troops. The Germans would come from four different directions. The Chetniks plan was to work in small groups, from 3 to 7 men and then attack from the sides (Flanks) of the Germans. However, the plan failed because troops disobeyed orders and threatened a frontal assault. Mihailovich travelled down to meet the men and was almost captured. Mihailovich managed to escape and the Chetniks were heavily defeated.

1942

After the failure of the operation, the USA has entered the war and began to support Yugoslavia and Mihailovich. Mihailovich is promoted to the position of General. In the spring of 1942, numbers increase in support of the Chetniks; radio stations are established, allowing Mihailovich to command troops across Yugoslavia. However, Mihailovich lacked in arms and equipment needed to attack the Germans.

September 1943

With British support, and the British and Americans had pushed into Italy, Mihailovich planned a large offensive against the Germans. They planned to push the Germans to one focal point and surround them on three sides of the city, with artillery bombardments placing pressure on the Germans.

The plan did not work, as the Communist Partisans switched sides and attacked Mikhailovich's forces on the rear. Mikhailovich's troops had to remove themselves from the attack, allowing the Germans to call reinforcements from Albania.

Partisans

Another resistance group emerged as well, the Partisans. They took their orders from Russia and therefore did not start involving themselves with the resistance movement until Operation Barbarossa. However, they had spent time sabotaging and training troops. By September 1941, Tito had built up an army of 70,000. They based themselves in the mountains of Montenegro. They were Communist, led by a man nicknamed Tito and first focused on building a base of operations and power. Tito was not only there to resist the Germans but also to build a future power base to install Communism and was using the German occupation as a rallying call for Communism. They used typical hit and run tactics and troops were ordered not to attack German groups which had larger numbers. The Partisans planned attacks on German groups, where there was a clear advantage of numbers and the ability to attack on familiar ground, such as the mountains. Discipline and winning the population over were essential. All food had to be paid for, and any looters were shot. Finally, they too had a propaganda campaign; posters, leaflets and the newspaper the 'Borba' were used to encourage support, resistance, recruitment and uprisings. Moscow even provided 'Radio Free Yugoslavia', which promoted Tito and Communism. In September 1941, the Partisans encouraged an uprising in Montenegro and pushed the Italian forces to the Adriatic Sea. They captured their weapons and released the 4,000 Italian prisoners.

By the end of 1943, the British were supporting the Partisans as well as the Soviet support. In the final days of the German occupation, the Partisans joined the Russians at the borders of Yugoslavia and joined in the invasion of Yugoslavia helping to drive out the Germans.

German operations and planning

In response to the guerrilla warfare, the Germans used both propaganda and extreme violence. They used wanted posters, which offered a 200,000-dinar reward for Mihailovich and 100,000 dinars for Tito, whilst continuing to inflict mass killings on local populations. The military attempted to encircle Mihailovich using four columns to surround the rebel forces in Operation Mihailovich as well as on later attempts to capture Mihailovich.

It has been estimated that the causalities for the killings during September 1941 and were in the region of 49,750, both civilian and military. Considering this lasted only a few months, this is a huge casualty total. Not only did the Germans attack civilians, but they also burnt villages and committed assassinations.

The Soviet Union and the guerrilla war in Chechnya.

This was a conflict between the Soviet Union and Chechenia rebels.

Background:

There were two phases or two wars between Chechnya and Russia. The First Chechen War was a war of nationalist independence from Russia, with religion. It took place between 1994 and 1996. In 1991 the Soviet Union had collapsed and changed from a communist state to a democracy. Certain states demanded and gained freedom. Chechnya had an unofficial party voted in as the largest party, and they were pro-separatist. After a failed coup by the Russian government, war broke out between the Russian government and the Chechen separatists. After a vicious struggle, Chechnya was granted independence, which was signed in August 1996.

Events and guerrilla warfare

The leaders of the Russian forces in Chechnya are corrupt, the soldiers are poorly trained, rarely paid and badly equipped. Consequently, they have no will to win.

The Chechens, on the other hand, were pursuing a centuries-old vow to drive the occupiers from their land, which is one of the many republics that make up the Russian Federation.

First, study the people. Second, know the territory. Third, study your opposition's weapons and equipment, and how they might employ this equipment in an urban environment. Finally, the Chechen force went into battle as light as possible.

"Each 75-man ambush group set up in buildings along one street block, and only on one side of the street—never on both sides of a street because of the crossfires a two-sided ambush would create. Only the lower levels of multi-story buildings were occupied to avoid casualties. One 25-man platoon comprised the "killer team" and set up in three positions along the target avenue. They had the responsibility for destroying whatever column entered their site. The other two 25-man platoons set up in the buildings at the assumed entry-points to the ambush site. They had responsibility for sealing off the ambush entry from escape by or reinforcement of the ambushed forces. The killer platoon established a command point (platoon HQ) with the centre squad. As the intended target column entered the site, the squad occupying the building nearest the entry point would contact the other two squads occupying the centre and far building positions. Primary means of communications was by Motorola radio. Once the lead vehicle into the site reached the far squad position, the far squad would contact the other two squads. The commander at the central squad would initiate or signal to initiate the ambush. Minefields were employed to reinforce ambushes by taking out reinforcing armour and to relieve pressure on the killer platoons in case the ambush bogged down."

Chechen Commander: On Urban Warfare in Chechnya, report from the US Marine Corps, 1999.

Understand the enemy

The Chechens were particularly skilled at urban combat. According to the Chechen military doctrine, it was important to understand the enemy in detail from a military and political sense, as well as a cultural sense. Chechen forces suffered only minimal psychological trauma, possibly in part because of their history of resistance to Russian control. Chechens also used civilians/non-combatants to exercise psychological deception. They declared to the Russians and general media that some villages and suburbs were pro-Russian or non-committed, when in fact these same areas were centres for strategic planning, command and control, and logistic purposes.

In urban combat, they did not rely on streets, signs, and most buildings as reference points. They instead used significant buildings and monuments instead because they usually remain intact. Chechen surveillance was done by day and attacked at night, which the Russians did not like to do.

The most effective weapon system employed against infantry was the sniper; nothing could slow down infantry as much as the sniper. One fighter could essentially tie down many men. Once the first shots were fired by the sniper, they could move away. The enemy would have stopped and would then have to search, and hopefully destroy, the sniper if they were still in their position. Snipers would also be used to set traps. They would draw the Russian troops towards a building. The route to the building would be set as a trap by other units.

The Chechen forces were very successful in redirecting Russian artillery and other fire onto Russian forces. Chechens would aim to get between two Russian positions/groups of men in the city, especially at night. They would fire in one direction and then the other before moving out of the area. The enemy thinking they were under attack, would fire at each other, and this could last for hours.

The movement was the key to success against the slower and heavier Russian force, in the opinion of the Chechen commander. The Chechens tried to confuse the Russians by moving behind and parallel to the Russian force once it entered the city. Snipers set up in hiding positions that supported their respective platoons. The Chechen commander described the ambushes/assaults in the following manner:

"U.S. Marine Corps Intelligence Activity analyst Arthur Speyer, speaking about the battle for Grozny to an audience at RAND, noted several Chechen weaknesses from a U.S. perspective. First, the greatest weakness of the Chechens was their inability to conduct an extensive engagement. The small size of the Chechen units, coupled with their limited ammunition supplies, caused them to avoid large-scale battles. The Russians discovered that drawing the Chechens into a long engagement would allow the Russian force the time to surround the position and use overwhelming fire support. Control was another problem for Chief of Staff Aslan Maskhadov. He stated that many of the independent groups decided for themselves when, where, and how long they would remain in combat. On more than one occasion Maskhadov noted that local militia forces would simply pick up and go home when they got bored, tired, or cold. Troops were required to withstand long periods of intense combat with limited re-supply and rest."

Chechen commanders were so concerned about secrecy that they did not tell their troops about their objective until they were on their way to the fighting.

Chechen commanders did not move by flanking. Instead it has been described as being like chess moves, where you aim to hit the Russians where they least expect it. They also used Hugging techniques, where you get so close to the enemy, they can't use their artillery without hitting their own men.

Weapons and equipment:

In urban (city) combat, the Chechen fighters used mortars effectively during the conflict but also feared enemy mortars more than any other weapon.

The favoured weapon of the Chechens was the Rocket Propelled Grenade launcher, known as an RPG. The destruction of Russian armour was a great psychological defeat for the Russians and a great morale booster to the Chechens.

Hand-held radios were the main communication device. There was one radio for every six fighters, but clearly, it would have been preferable to have one per combatant.

The Chechens were also very interested in capturing or obtaining Shmel. The Shmel is a Russian flamethrower. Flamethrowers were important because both sides realized that fire weapons were highly effective in urban warfare. Going into a building is dangerous; you don't know the plan for the building, people could be hiding around multiple corners or behind furniture. The tactic, like the one used in Operation Market Garden, was to burn the enemy out. They also can be used against vehicles and fortified positions as a breaching device.

Other lessons were learned:

The tracer round. This is a piece of ammunition that sets itself alight. When it hits a target, it burns brightly, effectively lighting up the area. There were found to be useless in urban areas due to serious negative trade-offs.

Unlike the Vietnam war, Chechens generally did not place mines or booby traps inside buildings. The possibility of friendly casualties was not worth any possible benefit.

In June 1995, the Budyonnovsk hospital hostage crisis took place; separatists took more than 1,500 people hostage in southern Russia. About 120 Russian civilians died before a ceasefire.

As the territory controlled by the Chechens shrank, the separatists used classic guerrilla warfare tactics, setting booby traps and mining roads in enemy-held territory. The successful use of makeshift explosives was very notable; they also effectively exploited a combination of mines and ambushes. Separatists resorted to mass-hostage takings, attempting to influence the Russian public and leadership.

Summary:

"The lessons learned by Chechen combatants are particular to that region, whilst others have wider applications. The significant and continuing lesson was that conventional armies want to avoid urban combat but increasing urbanization and the danger of strikes from high-precision weapons may well force the fight into the city, where the defender has all the advantages. The Chechen decision to continue to fight from successive cities shows their reliance on this tactic."

Chechen Commander: On Urban Warfare in Chechnya, this is from a report received from the US Marine Corps, 1999.

Chapter 8:

Amphibious Operations

***

This section will look at Amphibious Operations:

- World War 2: D-Day
- What was the Allies' plan?
- Deception: Operation Bodyguard
- US operations in 1945 Iwo Jima and Okinawa.
- Philippine Sea
- Leyte Gulf

D-Day

Background:

This was a battle between the USA, Britain and Germany, as well as other nations. The USA came into the war in December 1941 when Japan attacked the American Navy base at Pearl Harbor in Hawaii. Soon afterwards, Germany declared war on the USA. From 1942 onwards, large numbers of American troops arrived in Britain to prepare for what was called The Second Front: an invasion of German-occupied Europe along with the British.

The date fixed for the invasion was 6th June 1944. It was to be the biggest amphibious operation in history, involving thousands of planes and ships and hundreds of thousands of soldiers. The target was the coast of Normandy. All along the French coast, the Germans had spent several years constructing strong defences known as the Atlantic Wall.

Events:

In May 1943 planning began for the invasion of France.

In November 1943, Prime Minister Churchill and President Roosevelt met in Cairo, Egypt. The main outline of the plan was settled as well as the command structure.

By January 1944, detailed planning had started. To be successful, a big target area had to be selected, and many men were involved from day one of the invasion.

American General Eisenhower believed that the capture of Cherbourg was vital if the Allies were to supply their men with what they needed for a successful advance across France. The Americans planned an attack on five beaches and that each beach should be attacked by a national unit; therefore, command structures would be simplified. Two American units (Utah and Omaha), one to the Canadians (Juno) and two to the British (Sword and Gold).

The success of D-Day depended upon the soldiers that landed being regularly supplied as they advanced. To unload many troops and supplies by sea, a harbour was needed. The problem was that there was no place to land ships safely with enough supplies to do this. To solve this problem, the Allies came up with the idea of creating an artificial harbour that would be anchored near to the landing beaches but away from the German artillery. The artificial harbour that was built was codenamed 'Mulberry'. There were 12 miles of floating roadways in Mulberry Harbour. The floating roads were nicknamed 'Whales'. They also developed an oil pipeline called Pluto. Apart from Mulberry Harbour and Pluto, there were several other creative inventions used to help the Allied invasion.

The Allies' plan:

The most obvious part of the French coast to attack was the Pas De Calais, only 30 miles across the English Channel. However, this was the region most heavily defended by the Germans. Therefore, it was decided to land the invasion force further west in Normandy which was less well protected. The problem here was that this involved a longer sea crossing during which the invasion fleet could be attacked.

The Allies developed an elaborate hoax to trick the Germans into thinking that the Pas de Calais was their target. Many bombing raids were made there in the run-up to D-Day, and a phoney American army was created in Kent with dummy camps, tanks and ammunition dumps. They also sent many fake radio messages for this non-existent army because they knew the Germans would be listening in. The scheme worked. Hitler was convinced the Pas de Calais was where the Allies would land and made sure the best German units were stationed there.

Deception: Operation Bodyguard

Inflatable tanks were parked at ports in eastern and southern Britain for the Luftwaffe to photograph. Germany had many secret agents in Britain, but they had been turned by the British as part of the Double Cross System. Using the German agents that had been turned by the Allies, misinformation was fed to the Germans, some of which led the German army to expect an attack in either Norway or southern France instead of Normandy.

1945 USA combined operations in the Pacific Ocean

- Iwo Jima
- Okinawa
- Philippine Sea
- Leyte Gulf

Background:

The conflict between Japan and the US during World War Two began on 7th December 1941 with Pearl Harbor and ended with the dropping of the second atomic bomb on Japan (in Nagasaki) on 9th August 1945. The US began to retaliate against the Japanese after Pearl Harbor. They started to capture Japanese held territory. It was mostly Japanese and Thai forces against Australian, British, French and American forces.

Iwo Jima:

"Well, this will be easy. The Japanese will surrender Iwo Jima without a fight." Chester W. Nimitz

This was a battle between the USA and Japan. In February 1945 the bloodiest battle occurred, the Battle of Iwo Jima (a small island south of Japan) with an American victory. The island was roughly 575 miles from the Japanese coast and approximately 7.5 square miles in size. The island was sophisticated and easy to defend for many reasons. The volcano Mount Suribachi was on one end of the island. It stood at 550ft and contained the headquarters, miles of tunnels, artillery and even a radar station all hidden inside the mountain.

Iwo Jima was defended by about 23,000 Japanese army and navy troops. The Japanese fought from underground caves, dugouts, and tunnels that were difficult to find and destroy and were a total of 11 miles in length.

The island had been bombed by American warplanes for months before the Americans invaded. For three days before the Americans landed, the Navy bombarded the island with troops, vehicles and equipment.

To take the island, the operation would have to be an amphibious landing. At 10 am the US troops landed on the south-eastern point of the island, near Mount Suribachi. Initially, it looked like the island had been cleared due to the aerial and naval bombardment. For over an hour, thousands of men and supplies landed on the island's beaches and began moving inland. However, this was a trap, and the Japanese had deliberately made the Americans land without firing on them. It was an attack, which came from the left, right and in front of the Americans, which created huge casualties. Japanese General Tadamichi Kuribayashi had spent 9 months on the island and had made the entire island into a complex fortress, with almost all bunkers and defensive positions linked with tunnels, which the Americans were not aware of.

This meant that when Americans did attack and cleared the bunkers and other defensive positions, the Japanese were able to move back into the cleared area and begin attacking again. Although the entire system was not completed, it was still a massive task to defeat, and some of the areas had received enough supplies of fuel, food and water to last 3 months!

To counter the problems on the beach, American soldiers climbed from landing craft with grappling hooks and scaled a high ridge almost a mile in height. The aim was to fire on the enemy shooting at the Marine landings on the beaches below. The Americans were soon pinned down by heavy Japanese fire and engaged in non-stop fighting for 31 days before they could be relieved.

By, 11:30 the marines, without many vehicles, had come off the beach and had moved to the closest airfield.

Japan:	USA
General Tadamichi Kuribayashi	Admiral Chester W. Nimitz
20,530–21,060 troops	110,000 U.S. Marines, U.S. Soldiers, U.S. Navy corpsmen, USAAF personnel, and others Special and important Equipment: M2 flamethrowers
23 tanks	54 Tanks, 8 with flamethrowers.
438 artillery pieces	
33 naval guns	
69 anti-tank guns	
300 anti-aircraft guns	500+ ships

Unfortunately, thousands upon thousands died on both sides, and some say it was not worth all the bloodshed.

This island served as a U.S base after the battle.

Battle of the Philippine Sea June 15–20, 1944

This was a battle between the USA and Japan. In May 1942 American soldiers surrendered in the Philippines, so now the Japanese controlled almost all of South East Asia, with almost 50,000 POWs at their mercy who were dying every day from the horrible conditions.

The Japanese Plan

The overall aim was to destroy the American fleet in one decisive battle. It was a counterstrike against the Americans with the aim of stopping the Americans from taking the Mariana Islands. They, therefore, built a massive fleet of ships known as Operation Argo, which committed the entire Japanese fleet.

The Americans

They had planned for the attack to start on Saipan, with the aim of bringing American bombers in range of Japan. due to the American Radar systems, which detected the Japanese incoming aircraft.

Japan: Admiral Koga	USA Admiral Sprunance
Roughly 96,000 troops	Roughly 500, 000 troops
5 fleet carriers 4 light carriers 5 battleships 13 cruisers 31 destroyers 24 submarines	7 fleet carriers 8 light carriers 7 battleships 21 cruisers 68 destroyers 28 submarines
900 aircraft	750 aircraft

The battle

The beginning of the battle was locating the ships, and the aircraft began to engage each other. The Japanese were no match for the American pilots and were shot down in great numbers.

Another wave of Japanese aircraft attacked various groups of ships but did little damage to the American ships.

American submarines had sighted the Japanese carriers and fired torpedoes, disabling one, which later exploded due to the fuel vapours released by the torpedo hit, and destroyed the other with its first spread of torpedoes.

Another set of American aircraft went in search of the Japanese fleet, with the aim of attacking its carriers.

In total, the Japanese lost 3 carriers, over 480 planes and 3,000 dead.

In total, the Americans lost 1 battleship, over 125 planes and 100 dead.

Leyte Gulf

This was a battle between the USA and Japan. In October 1944 the largest naval battle in history took place, the Battle of Leyte Gulf, fought near the Philippines, with American troops invading the Philippines and winning. This was the first time that the Japanese organised planned kamikaze attacks as they did not have many planes.

The Japanese Plan:

The plan was to destroy the American naval fleet and to stop the invasion of the Philippines by seeking out the American fleet and destroying them. The main fleet was stationed in and near Singapore. Troops were brought in from China and were ready to be deployed from the mainland to the Philippines in amphibious landings. The aircraft carriers had to be rebuilt and were based in Japan. The Japanese also based their planning around 4 key areas known as Sho (Sho 1 to 4) which were based in northern Japan, central Japan, the islands south of Japan and the Philippines. Each area represented a different Sho. The idea was that wherever the attack came from these different groups could meet at the point of attack, with the hope that the Americans would be overwhelmed and annihilated.

The American Plan:

To invade the island of Leyte. This would then be used as a base to attack and capture the rest of the Philippines (Operation King Two). One group of ships would lead the landings, two aircraft carriers would support the landing with air cover, and two support groups would protect the flanks of the landings from any Japanese counterattack. However, the Americans did not think that the Japanese would offer such an attack at sea, or that the island was so well defended.

Japan:	USA
General Mitsuru Ushijima	Admiral Chester W. Nimitz
Roughly 96,000 troops	Roughly 500, 000 troops
7 battleships 16 cruiser, 26 destroyers 3 Carriers	40 carries, 18 battleships, 200 destroyers, 300 support ships.

The Battle:

The first part of the battle was the Americans attacking the islands south of Japan using their aircraft carrier planes. These islands were known as Sho – 3, and the Japanese were ready. However, the Japanese pilots were poorly trained (200 hours for Japanese vs 350 hours of training time for American pilots) and lacked combat experience. As a result, the Americans inflicted heavy damage. The situation was made worse when the commander of the Japanese Carriers in Sho – 2 felt that this was a great time to send his fighters against the American carriers. Two destroyers were damaged, and over 500 Japanese fighters were destroyed.

After this, the Japanese started preparations for moving all troops, ships and aircraft to the Philippines. The Americans began bombarding Leyte Gulf, and the Carriers moved south for both the Americans and Japanese. The Japanese carriers were tasked not with attacking the Americans but attempting to get the American carrier to chase them away from the Leyte Gulf. The Japanese fleets from Singapore and Japan came together on the opposite side of the Leyte Gulf, and their aim was to go through the islands in a pincer movement, north and south of Leyte Gulf, and then attack the landing Americans and the fleet anchored offshore. The aircraft based on the north of the island would join in the attack at Leyte Gulf.

The attack began to falter. The Japanese ships heading south were spotted by American submarines, and three ships were sunk. The Japanese aircraft sent to attack the carriers took heavy casualties and only damaged a light cruiser.

In the north, Americans sent aircraft against the Northern Japanese fleet, destroying one battleship and one heavy destroyer, and losing 18 aircraft. However, the American pilots came back and gave the impression that they had destroyed/neutralised the northern fleet.

On October 25, the carriers coming from Japan had found the American carriers and launched 70 aircraft. It was the last attack by Japanese pilots and they sank nothing, with only a handful of survivors. The only thing left was for the Japanese to work as a decoy, which they were, and the Americans did chase them, leaving no protection or block to the Northern Japanese fleet. The Americans felt that the Japanese fleet coming from the north was no longer a threat and did not know that the Japanese carriers were useless, so they proceeded to chase the carriers.

The southern Japanese fleet had been spotted on October 24[th.] The Americans prepared by placing a huge number of ships in a P shaped formation. Because the entry to Leyte Gulf was narrow the Japanese ships would come in single file, one in front of the other, limiting their ability to fire. However, because the Americans were in a P shape, they would be able to fire at the Japanese from all sides and use the element of surprise. The greatest firepower from a ship would be from its side, which meant that all American ships in the south were set into that position. For the Japanese to do the same, they would have to manoeuvre into position, by which time they would be destroyed. The American plan started with 5 American destroyers attacking the left and right sides of the Japanese ships with torpedoes, sinking 3 destroyers and one battleship. The Japanese were reduced to 3 ships, a battleship, and two destroyers. The American ships waiting in a line fired more than 4,000 rounds, and after 5 minutes all the ships were destroyed. Three ships did make a retreat but were destroyed by aircraft the next day.

In the north, the Japanese had started to move south to the Leyte Gulf. At 7 am the Japanese encountered the Americans, and the Japanese made a colossal mistake. They began to attack at random, instead of forming a battle line, which caused complete chaos. The American Admiral launched his aircraft; his carriers were told to start producing smoke and move away at top speed. The four American destroyers attacked and were so aggressive that it caused further chaos for the Japanese. The Japanese had lost four destroyers and had utterly lost tactical control; he ordered the Japanese to withdraw and regroup. The aggressive attacks were so intense that the Japanese thought there was a stronger force than they had realised. They had also been misinformed that another American fleet was moving in from the north and that the Japanese fleet in the south had been destroyed. After two hours, Kamikaze pilots began to fly into the American carriers, damaging six and destroying one carrier. This was significant when compared to the Japanese fleet's attack that had only destroyed one and damaged two.

The decoy fleet in the north, the Japanese carriers, were all sunk by the end of the day.

Okinawa: Operation Iceberg

This was a battle between the USA, Britain and Japan. This was part of the reason for dropping atomic bombs on mainland Japan. The island of Okinawa was considered part of the plan to invade the home islands of Japan, as it connected to the main island itself. The island is 70 miles long and 7 miles wide. The island faced the largest amphibious landing of the Pacific War, and the US Navy had not lost this many ships since Pearl Harbor. 3,000 humans a day were killed, and the two atomic bombs dropped on Japan did not kill as many Japanese.

The Japanese Plan:

Like Iwo Jima, the Japanese had built interconnected tunnel systems, which linked strategic defences, and these fortifications were away from the beaches.

The Japanese planned two fronts. One front of attack was on land, and the other involved kamikaze tactics, at sea and in the air.

The island forces had retreated to the northern part of the island known as the Motobu peninsular, where the Japanese developed similar tactics to the ones used on Iwo Jima. Tunnel systems were connected to multiple hills or a system of tunnels inside a single hill. To the south, the Japanese had also built similar defences in and around the capital of the island Shuri.

The American Plan:

American Phase One:

This was to attack and neutralise the surrounding islands around the Japanese island of Okinawa.

American Phase Two:

This was amphibious landings on islands near to Okinawa, then further landings on Okinawa. This would end when the southern part of the island was captured.

American Phase Three:

This was the final securing of Okinawa in the North.

The Battle:

Landing on Okinawa, Hagushi, happened on April 1st, 1945. 1,300 ships were involved in the landing. 44,000 shells were fired on the beach before the landing. At 8 am, over an 8-mile front, the Americans began to land. By nightfall, over 60,000 troops had landed, two airfields had been captured, and the central part of the island had been captured.

By the 6th of April, most of the Island had been taken, but the defence by the Japanese had only just begun. The Americans began to realise that the Japanese had dug into surrounding hills and in the Motobu Peninsula. The Motobu Peninsula was to be the biggest obstacle faced by the Americans. On the same day, the Japanese began their air offensive, and 2 waves of fighters and kamikaze fighters attacked the American ships landing in Hagushi.

This was one of the bloodiest battles of the Pacific and ended on the 2nd of June, 1945. By the end of the fighting, over 400 US ships had been sunk, over 700 aircraft had been lost, and 200 tanks had been destroyed. The Japanese had lost 18 ships, 1,400 aircraft and 27 tanks had been destroyed. There were approximately 135,000 to 160,000 casualties in total. At least 52,000 Allied troops and 84,166–117,000 Japanese troops were killed. Of the 300,000 Okinawans, 149,425 were killed, committed suicide or went missing.

Chapter 9:

Airborne Operations, World War 2

***

This section will look at Airborne Operations:

- World War 2: Arnhem
- So near, yet so far:

Arnhem. 1944 – 1945.

The Battle of Arnhem, Operation Market Garden (1944)

Background:

This was a battle between the Allies (mainly Britain and USA) and Germany during World War Two. During the operation, the British 1st Airborne Division and the Polish 1st Parachute Brigade were tasked with securing the bridge at Arnhem. The units were parachuted and glider-landed into the area in September. Later the main force was dropped almost too far from the bridge and never made all their objectives. A small number of the British 1st Airborne managed to get to the bridge but were unable to secure both sides.

Intelligence warning:

The 1st Allied Airborne Army, including one British and two American divisions, had been kept in reserve since the D-Day. Due to good weather conditions, their skills and training could be used.

Tony Hibbert was Brigade Major of the 1st Parachute Brigade: *"My first reaction was one of enormous enthusiasm and excitement because this was the first time that anyone on our side, had contemplated the proper strategic use of airborne forces en masse."*

The troops parachuted in near the Dutch towns of Eindhoven, Nijmegen and Arnhem, with the aim of taking the eight essential bridges. The planners called this an 'airborne carpet', which was slowly being chased by the advancing British tanks of 30 corps could push through to Germany.

The airborne commander, General Browning, had seven days to prepare. The information he was that there were two SS Panzer divisions near Arnhem, with many tanks and vehicles. This was very worrying as the British would potentially struggle to fight against a unit with this level of armour.

Major Tony Hibbert: *"He showed me photographs of German Panzer 4's; mainly I think they were tucked in underneath woods. He went to General Browning, and said that in his view the operation could not succeed, because of the presence of these two divisions."*

Day one

On Sunday the 17th of September, 500 gliders and 1,500 aircraft took off for their objectives. As the aircraft flew over, the Allied artillery fired on the Germans guarding the road ahead.

Major Tony Hibbert remembers: *"... an enormous feeling of excitement, and I think everyone at that stage felt totally confident they would win. Certainly, the flight over from England was absolutely beautiful. There was an absolute mass, an armada as far as the eye could see, in both directions, and about 20 planes wide, the most extraordinary sight I've ever seen."*

The American and British gliders and parachutists drifted down on target and began to move towards the bridges they had to take. The road which 30 corps travelled was just wide enough for two vehicles to pass. This made it easy for the German infantry to defend as they only had to attack the front of the column. As the tanks approached, German infantry picked off the leading nine vehicles. This would bring the whole column to a stop and would take on average 40 minutes before they moved again.

The British paratroopers advanced towards Arnhem but were soon under attack. They also found that their radios didn't work properly. As a result, it was impossible to coordinate the attack or defence properly. However, one group of British troops did find a way through the German defences. By 8 pm on the first day, the Allies had captured the northern end of the bridge across the Rhine. American troops had reached their objectives, but most of the bridges had been destroyed by the Germans before they could be captured.

At the end of the first day, 30 corps had only advanced seven miles from their start point and had not reached the first bridges. While this took place, the Germans were reinforcing, and their tanks were moving into Arnhem.

The second day and third day: So near, yet so far:

On the 18th of September, corps began to make progress. Their tanks made 20 miles in a few hours, meeting with the Americans at one of the intact bridges. On the third day, they reached Nijmegen, but the Americans were still fighting in the streets to reach the bridge across the River Waal.

Once they had taken the bridge, only Arnhem was left, and the north end at least was still in British hands. However, they could not get across the bridge.

Moffat Burriss *"The bullets hitting the water looked like a hailstorm, kicking up little spouts of water. When we reached about the halfway point, then the mortar and artillery fire started falling. And when a boat was hit with an artillery shell or a mortar shell, it just disintegrated, and everybody was lost."*

The Americans decided to make a daring dash across the river in any boats they could find, and anything they could use to paddle, including their rifles! Half of the Americans were killed or wounded on the crossing. The survivors reached the far bank and stormed the bridge. However, once the tanks crossed, they halted, waiting for an anti-tank gun battery to be destroyed. This meant that it was too late for the British parachute battalion at the north end of the bridge at Arnhem. The Germans had moved their tanks into Arnhem, and one by one they were demolishing the houses the British were using for their defence. By now the British Para troops had few anti-tank weapons, no food, and little ammunition.

Major Tony Hibbert remembers the German tanks: *"We really had nothing we could do to them, and they drove up and down the street, firing high explosive into the side of the building, to create the gap, and then firing smoke shells through that. The phosphorus from the smoke shells burned us out. By about 8 o'clock, on Wednesday evening, the fires got out of control and of course, we had by this time about 300 wounded in the cellars."*

Eventually, the Allies were forced to abandon the bridge and tried to escape. British Para troops were holding the village of Oosterberck, three miles from Arnhem. By now 30 corps, commanded by General Horrocks, was on the other side of the river from the airborne troops. They could not, however, cross and German artillery controlled the river.

Operation Market Garden failed.

The British force at the bridge eventually surrendered on September 21st, and a full withdrawal of the remaining forces was made on September 26th. The British evacuated the 2,500 British survivors. The Parachute division left 6,500 wounded and 1,500 dead. It would be four months before the Allies crossed the Rhine again and captured the German industrial heartland. As for the war, it continued and dragged on, costing the lives of many thousands of civilians and servicemen.

As a tribute, the rebuilt bridge was renamed 'John Frost-bridge' after the commander of the paratroopers.

Chapter 10:

Atom Bomb

***

This section will look at Atom Bombs and their use:

- Reasons for dropping atom bombs in 1945
- The Bombing of Hiroshima

Reasons for dropping atom bombs in 1945. Were the Americans right to nuclear bomb Japan?

Albert Einstein: *"The splitting of the atom has changed everything except the way we think. Thus we drift toward unparalleled catastrophe. We shall require a substantially new manner of thinking if mankind is to survive."*

George Wald, *"Dropping those atomic bombs on Hiroshima and Nagasaki was a war crime."*

J. Robert Oppenheimer, *"Now I am become Death, the destroyer of Worlds."*

President Harry S. Truman, *"The atom bomb was no 'great decision.' It was merely another powerful weapon in the arsenal of righteousness."*

Dropping the Bomb saved a lot of lives in Japan. Paul Tibbets. *"I got into the air corps to defend the United States to the best of my ability. That's what I believe in, and that's what I work for. Number two, I'd had so much experience with airplanes... I'd had jobs where there was no particular direction about how you do it and then, of course, I put this thing together with my own thoughts on how it should be because when I got the directive, I was to be self-supporting at all times.*

On the way to the target, I was thinking: I can't think of any mistakes I've made. Maybe I did make a mistake: maybe I was too damned assured. At 29 years of age I was so shot in the ass with confidence I didn't think there was anything I couldn't do. Of course, that applied to airplanes and people. So, no, I had no problem with it. I knew we did the right thing because when I knew we'd be doing that, I thought, yes, we're going to kill a lot of people, but by God, we're going to save a lot of lives. We won't have to invade [Japan]."

https://www.theguardian.com/world/2002/aug/06/nuclear.japan

Background:

☢ This was a conflict between the 🇺🇸 USA and 🎌 Japan. To end World War II, the United States decided to drop an atomic bomb on the Japanese Mainland. The war in Europe had concluded when Nazi Germany signed its surrender on May 8th, 1945.

Events:

The first bomb was codenamed 'Fat Man'. It was detonated over the Japanese city of Nagasaki by the United States on 9 August 1945.

Two bombs were dropped, one on Hiroshima and one on Nagasaki three days later. Immediately after the second nuclear bomb, Japan surrendered, and WW2 was finally over. The United States dropped atomic bombs on the cities of Hiroshima and Nagasaki, during the final stage of the Second World War. The two bombs killed at least 129,000 people and are the only military combat use of nuclear weapons.

In the last year of the war, the Allies organised for the invasion of the Japanese mainland. Before the dropping of the bombs, the U.S. firebombed many Japanese cities. The Japanese, facing the same fate as the Nazis, refused to accept the Allies' demands for unconditional surrender. The Japanese choose to ignore it.

⚛ On the 6th of August, the U.S. dropped a uranium atomic bomb known as Little Boy on Hiroshima. The American President Harry S. Truman called for Japan's surrender and warned them to *"expect a rain of ruin from the air, the like of which has never been seen on this earth."* On the 9th of August, the U.S. dropped a plutonium atomic bomb known as Fat Man on Nagasaki. Within the first 2 to 4 months of the bombings, the radiation effects killed roughly 90,000–146,000 people in Hiroshima and 39,000–80,000 in Nagasaki, and roughly half of the deaths in each city occurred on the first day. The later deaths were from the effects of burns, radiation sickness, and malnutrition. In both cities, most of the dead were civilians, although Hiroshima had a sizable military garrison.

The Bombing of Hiroshima

Evidence:

1. The American army had produced 500,000 purple heart medals (given to soldiers who are wounded or killed in action) this was in preparation for the invasion of Japan. This was what they believed the casualty figures would be.
2. Every month between 1937 and the dropping of the bomb, between 100,000 and 200,000 Chinese were killed by the Japanese.
3. The Americans spent over $2bn (equivalent to $25bn today) developing nuclear weapons.
4. Japanese people believed it was dishonourable to surrender.
5. By the end of WW2 Japan had around 10 million Chinese in forced labour camps.
6. American troops had been moving through the Pacific towards Japan island-by-island with huge losses.
7. Even after the surrender, some Japanese military leaders tried to continue the fighting
8. There were around 100,000 Allied prisoners of war being held by the Japanese.

However, the detonation of the bomb will (you think) cause the death of 80,000 Japanese civilians and injure another 40,000. Many will die instantly, evaporated in the heat, others will gradually get sick from the radiation and die months or years later.

Generations from now, children in Japan will be born with birth defects caused by the radiation poisoning of their ancestors.

You also are receiving some reports that the Japanese are already on the point of surrender after you have successfully cut off their fuel supplies, they are no longer able to operate their tanks nor sea power.

Yoshitaka Kawamoto was thirteen years old. **He was in the classroom at Zakoba-cho, 0.8 kilometres away from the hypocentre.** *"Survivor One of my classmates, I think his name is Fujimoto, he muttered something and pointed outside the window, saying, "A B-29 is coming." He pointed outside with his finger. So I began to get up from my chair and asked him, "Where is it?" Looking in the direction that he was pointing towards, I got up on my feet, but I was not yet in an upright position when it happened. All I can remember was a pale lightning flash for two or three seconds. Then, I collapsed. I don't know much time passed before I came to. It was awful, awful. The smoke was coming in from somewhere above the debris. Sandy dust was flying around. . .*

I crawled over the debris, trying to find someone who was still alive. Then, I found one of my classmates lying alive. I held him up in my arms. It is hard to tell; his skull was cracked open, his flesh was dangling out from his head. He had only one eye left, and it was looking right at me. . . . he told me to go away.

I, so, was running, hands were trying to grab my ankles, they were asking me to take them along. I was only a child then. And I was horrified at so many hands trying to grab me. I was in pain, too. So all I could do was to get rid of them, it's terrible to say, but I kicked their hands away. I still feel bad about that. I went to Miyuki Bridge to get some water. At the river bank, I saw so many people collapsed there. . . I was small, so I pushed on the river along the small steps. The water was dead people. I had to push the bodies aside to drink the muddy water. We didn't know anything about radioactivity at that time. I stood up in the water and so many bodies were floating away along the stream."

Chapter 11:

The Cold War

✱✱✱

This section will look at Atom Bombs and their use or lack of use during the Cold War:

- The Cold War
- The nuclear arms race
- The arms race 1945-60
- ICBMs
- Mutual Assured Destruction (MAD Theory)
- The arms race 1960-91
- MIRVs
- Détente and Arms Reduction Talks
- Attempts at arms limitation
- End of the Arms Race

The Cold War:

☢ This was a series of conflicts and proxy wars between the ▬ USA and the ▬ USSR/Soviet Union. The Cold War was one of tension and proxy wars (also referred to in this book as Hot Spots) between the remaining superpowers from World War II: The United States and the Soviet Union. The United States and Russia had huge amounts of tension caused by a variety of issues, which have been touched upon in this book. These include World War 2, D-Day, and Atomic Bombs.

The nuclear arms race:

The Cold War was a conflict between the US and the USSR, which lasted from 1945 to 1991. It featured a nuclear arms race during where each superpower developed more advanced weapons.

The arms race 1945-60:

The nuclear arms race was fundamental to the Cold War. This was in part because of the belief that the more nuclear weapons you had, the more powerful you were. Both America and Russia created stockpiles of nuclear weapons. Many countries feared that the arms race within the Cold War was going in the direction of potentially total world destruction.

Both America and the USSR spent billions and billions of dollars trying to build up huge stockpiles. Towards the end of the Cold War, the Soviet Union was spending 27% of its country's budget on the military. This was too much for their economy and was crippling it, which helped to bring an end to the Cold War.

1949

☢ The Soviet Union successfully tested its own atomic bomb.

In the 1950s the Soviet Union produced medium-range ballistic missiles (MRBMs) and intermediate-range ballistic missiles (IRBMs). The aim was to use these missiles to support troops during the war. However, they could only be used against the United States if the Soviet Union had a nuclear base in that area.

1952

American President Truman then ordered a new, more powerful weapon to be built. The hydrogen bomb was successfully tested. This bomb was smaller than the Hiroshima bomb but 2,500 times more powerful.

1953

The Russians produced their own H-bomb.

USA produced a bomber called the B52 that could fly 6,000 miles and deliver a nuclear payload.

1957

In October, the first every satellite named Sputnik was launched from the Soviet Union. This led to missiles that could fly over continents, thus the name Inter-Continental Ballistic Missiles (ICBMs).

At the end of the decade, it was estimated that if Russia had attacked the US with nuclear missiles, 20 million Americans would have died and 22 million would be injured. America overcame this problem by developing the Minuteman missile. The missile stored its fuel in the engines, and it was now possible to fire a missile in thirty seconds. These missiles were also small (54 ft long and 10 ft in diameter) and could be stored under the ground, to protect them from attack.

Inter-Continental Ballistic Missiles: (ICBM)

In the 1950s both countries developed Intercontinental Ballistic Missiles or ICBMs. These missiles could be launched from as far away as 3,500 miles.

Both countries began to work on defences such as large radar arrays to tell if a missile had been launched. They also worked on defence missiles that could shoot down ICBMs.

Mutually Assured Destruction also known as M.A.D:

One of the major factors for creating a Cold War was termed Mutually Assured Destruction or M.A.D. This meant that both countries could destroy each other. The first strike was not important because the other side could still retaliate and destroy the country that had attacked first. Because of this, neither side ever used nuclear weapons as the cost would be too high.

This theory had two very contrasting effects:

- Mutual destruction caused the two superpowers to continue to develop more powerful nuclear weapons to maintain this idea of balance and threat.

- At the same time, it acted as a deterrent. No side would want to strike first as it would destroy itself as well.

Other Countries were involved:

During the Cold War, three other nations Britain, France, and the People's Republic of China developed their own nuclear bomb and weapons.

As the USA and USSR continued to stockpile weapons, countries around the world grew increasingly tense. American Allies were subject to propaganda about the evils of Communism – the Russian system of government. The fear was real!

The arms race from 1960 to 1991:

By 1961, there were enough atomic bombs to destroy the world. Russia put their money into producing more missiles, regardless of quality, while America built fewer but better-quality missiles. The Atlas missile could fly at 5,000 miles at 16,000 miles per hour. Nonetheless, the emphasis was put on new weapon systems, such as mobile missile launchers, missiles stored in the underground in missile silos, and in 1960 the first Polaris submarine was launched carrying 16 nuclear missiles. Each one of the Polaris missiles carried four warheads which could target separate cities. One submarine effectively carried 64 nuclear warheads. In 1967, China exploded an H-bomb. China was a communist country. In the west, NATO felt outnumbered as the table below shows and so had to place their faith in nuclear missiles. Other important developments included:

Submarine-launched ballistic missiles (SLBMs):

This is a Submarine that could fire ballistic missiles (SLBMs) which had the advantage in that they could be launched from the sea.

Multiple independently-targeted re-entry vehicles (MIRVs):

Multiple independently-targeted re-entry vehicles which were missiles with several warheads which could be fired at different targets.

Détente and Arms Reduction Talks:

While the Arms Race continued, tension built, and it became very expensive for both American and the USSR. By the 1970s, both sides recognised that something had to change. The two sides began to talk, and tensions began to calm down between the two countries.

By the early 1980s, there was parity between the two superpowers in the development of nuclear weapons. By 1981, the US had 8,000 ICBMs and the USSR 7,000 ICBMs.

ICBMs	Planes capable of carrying nuclear weapons
USA 8,000	USA 4,000
Soviet Union 7,000	Soviet Union 5,000

However, by 1983, the US President, Ronald Reagan, changed the whole balance of the nuclear arms race with the Strategic Defence Initiative (S.D.I.), also known as Star Wars. America was determined to win the Cold War and believed that Russia could be forced to disarm with S.D.I.

Star Wars took the Cold War to space. It proposed a defence system, which would stop Soviet nuclear bombs from reaching America. The plan was to launch an army of satellites equipped with powerful lasers, and missiles, which could intercept and destroy Soviet missiles in space. President Reagan believed that 'Star Wars' technology would make Soviet nuclear missiles useless and force the USSR to disarm. This proved to be a defining moment in the arms race.

Détente:

This was a period of calming tensions between the two superpowers. Both sides became evenly matched and after the Cuban missile crisis in 1962 worked together to limit the growth of nuclear stockpiles. The strategic defence initiative was a break from this policy. Soviet leaders knew that they could not compete with Reagan's Star Wars plan. The Russians were behind the USA in space and computer technology whilst the Soviet economy was not good enough to fund even more defence spending.

To try to slow down the spending of the Arms Race, both countries agreed to reduce arms through talks called SALT I and SALT II. SALT stood for Strategic Arms Limitation Talks.

Attempts at arms limitation:

After 1960, there were several attempts to reduce nuclear weapons.

This was for several reasons:

1. In the 1950s there was more awareness of the potential threat of nuclear warfare and the destruction of the world. Groups including the Campaign for Nuclear Disarmament (CND) organised protest marches and did much to publicise the dangers of nuclear warfare.

2. In October 1962 the world experienced the Cuban Missile Crisis. The superpowers came very close to nuclear war when American President, Kennedy, ordered a blockade of Cuba to prevent Soviet ships containing nuclear missiles for Cuban missile sites. Thankfully for the planet, Russian leader Khrushchev ordered the ships to turn around as the two leaders reached a compromise. To reduce tensions, the two countries set up a red phone/hotline and began arms limitation talks.

3. The later 1960s and 1970s were known as detente with both superpowers working to agree to arms limitations.

4. The USA and the Soviet Union needed to find ways of reducing their budgets. A major cause was the number of nuclear weapons and military and having to maintain it. For the Soviet Union, it was one of the major causes that the USSR had a crippled economy.

5. 1963 Partial Test Ban Treaty. This treaty was signed by over 100 countries and banned all nuclear explosions except those underground. Over 100 countries signed.

6. 1968 Non-proliferation Treaty. The treaty was signed by non-nuclear nations. They agreed not to develop nuclear weapons whilst countries with nuclear weapons agreed to negotiate to reduce the number of nuclear weapons. It was signed by over 100 countries.

The 1970s

1. 1972 SALT 1(Strategic Arms Limitations Talks)

The USA and USSR agreed to limit certain types of nuclear weapons. However, no limits were placed on delivery systems, so the arms race continued. This was a good first step.

2. 1979 SALT 2

The USA and USSR agreed to limit certain types of nuclear missiles. However, there was no agreement for the delivery systems, and the USA refused to approve SALT 2 after the Soviets invaded Afghanistan in 1979.

The 1980s

1. 1982-3 START Strategic Arms Limitation Talks

The USA and USSR met in Geneva, Switzerland but this was a period of tension between the superpowers, as a result, the Soviet Union withdrew from the talks in 1983.

2. 1987 Intermediate Nuclear Forces Treaty (INF)

The INF abolished nuclear missiles, conventional ground-launched ballistic missiles and cruise missiles, which had ranges of 500-5500 kilometres. This was to be completed by 1 June 1991. Both countries could inspect each other's military installations.

End of the Arms Race:

This came to an end along with the financial and political collapse of the USSR in 1991, and with it the Cold War.

Cold war CFE Treaty, 1990: The Treaty on Conventional Armed Forces.

The Treaty was a arms limitation agreement between the Soviet Union, and the Warsaw Pact vs the United States and her NATO allies. The organisation of this treaty began in the last years of the Cold War; however, the treaty itself has its origins going back to 1972. The treaty was signed by George Bush Snr and Mikhail Gorbachev. It came into effect in 1992. It limited the number of convential troops that any country could have, with the aim of continuing the stability in the region.

They were limited to 20,000 tanks, 6,800 aircraft, 2,000 helicopters with around 275,000 troops.

These forces were then limited to zones. The idea was that this would make the build-up of troops extremely difficult, while also encouraging transparency and the exchange of data between the two parties.

Chapter 12:

21st Century Warfare

***

This section will look at Atom Bombs and their use, or lack of use, during the Cold War:
- Warfare at the beginning of the twenty-first century
- Impact of terrorism
- Different types of terrorist acts
- 9/11
- High tech weapons
- The arms race 1960-91
- MIRVs
- Détente and Arms Reduction Talks
- Attempts at arms limitation
- End of the Arms Race

Warfare at the beginning of the twenty-first century:

The greatest change at the beginning of the twenty-first century was the impact of terrorism. Terrorists were now in a position and were willing to use civilians as targets. This was seen to great effect with the 9/11 attacks and the subsequent attacks after the Second Gulf War.

Impact of terrorism:

Terrorism is an instrument of war that greatly increased in the second half of the twentieth century. It is used as a means of coercion, or to create fear, and deliberately targets areas regarded as safe for civilians.

Different types of terrorist acts:

Kidnappings and hostage-taking

Terrorists use kidnapping and hostage-taking to start a position and to blackmail or negotiate their wants and needs.

Hijackings and skyjackings

A hijacking is a seizure by force of a vehicle based on land, along with its passengers, and/or its cargo. A skyjacking is the taking of an aircraft, which creates a mobile hostage barricade situation.

Armed attacks and assassinations

There are attacks, which include raids and ambushes. Assassinations are the killing of a selected victim, usually by bombings, snipers or small arms.

Significant terrorist organisations:

This section will look at some of the most significant terrorist organisations of the second half of the twentieth century. They were mostly in the Middle East. They included:

The Popular Front for the Liberation of Palestine (PFLP).

This was set up in 1968 to attack targets outside Israel with skyjackings. This is boarding a plane and hijacking it, then holding passengers to ransom or blowing up the plane. The height of their skyjackings took place in 1970 when they seized four airlines, three of which were flown to Dawson's Field in Jordan where they were blown up in front of the world's media.

The PFLP has taken a hard line on Palestinian national goals, opposing the more moderate stance of other groups and political parties. The PFLP has and continues to oppose negotiations with the Israeli government and favours a one-state solution to the Israeli–Palestinian conflict.

The one state solution still has many forms, but the premise is that Israel and Palestine become one state, with one federal government to run the country, thus uniting Palestine and Israel.

Palestine Liberation Organization (PLO).

This is a secular, revolutionary, Palestinian, Marxist-Leninist and socialist organization. It was founded in 1967 and has constantly been the second-largest of the groups.

Black September.

This was a terrorist organisation that carried out a terrorist attack at the 1972 Munich Olympics which led to the death of Israeli hostages.

The Black September Organization was a Palestinian terrorist organization and was founded in 1970. They were responsible for the fatal kidnapping and murder of eleven Israeli Olympic athletes, officials and a West German policeman. It was their most publicised event. These events led to the creation of permanent, professional, and military-trained counter-terrorism forces of major European countries, and the reorganization and specialization of already standing units like the Special Air Service of the UK.

Hezbollah

Hezbollah, which means 'Party of God' is an Islamic terrorist group and political party founded in Lebanon shortly after that country's 1982 civil war. The group has kidnapped Israeli soldiers, carried out missile attacks and suicide bombings against Israeli military and civilian targets.

Hezbollah was conceived by Muslim clerics and was primarily formed to resist the Israeli occupation. It was funded by Iran following the Israeli invasion of Lebanon in 1982.

Hezbollah has grown to an organization with seats in the Lebanese government, a radio and a satellite TV station, social services and large-scale military deployment of fighters beyond Lebanon's borders.

In 2000, at the end of the Israeli occupation of South Lebanon, Hezbollah's military strength grew significantly, such that its paramilitary wing is considered more powerful than the Lebanese Army. Currently, Hezbollah receives military training, weapons, and financial support from Iran, and political support from Syria.

The Irish Republican Army (IRA)

Background:

There had been tensions in Ireland ever since the English invaded the country and attempted to take control of it, both through religion and violence. After World War One, British Prime Minister David Lloyd George decided that a solution to the troubles in Northern Ireland would be to split the country in two. The Catholics would have most of the country, and the Protestants would have what is now Northern Ireland.

Events:

The original Irish Republican Army (IRA) fought a guerrilla war against British rule in Ireland in the Irish War of Independence, 1919–1921.

By 1968, the Northern Ireland parliament had been dominated by Unionists for over fifty years. Unionists are people who want Northern Ireland to remain a part of Britain. The government attempted to solve social and political ills, such as discrimination against Catholics. However, they were too slow for Nationalists and Republicans and too quick for many Unionists. This gave rise to growing tension and violence between the two communities.

The increasing disorder caused the UK governments to intercede. In 1969, the situation was so bad that British troops were sent in. By 1972, the British government suspended the Northern Ireland parliament and imposed direct rule from Westminster.

The Irish Republican Army (IRA) used various tactics including numerous bombings in both Northern Ireland and on the British mainland. The British retaliated with force and torture was claimed to have taken place.

I.R.A. Green Book: *"A member of the I.R.A. is such by his own choice, his convictions were the only factor which compels him to volunteer, his objectives the political freedom and social and economic justice for his people. Apart from the few minutes in the career of the average Brit that he comes under attack, the Brit has no freedom or personal initiative. He is told when to sleep, where to sleep when to get up, where to spend his free time etc."*

The Strategy is:

1. A war of attrition, which was aimed at causing as many casualties and deaths as possible, which would create demand from UK citizens for the British withdrawal.

2. A bombing campaign will be aimed at making the enemy's financial interest in our country unprofitable while at the same time curbing long-term financial investment in our country.

3. To make the Six Counties as at present and for the past several years ungovernable except by colonial military rule.

4. To use propaganda and publicity campaigns to sustain the war and gain support.

5. To punish criminals, collaborators and informers.

Hamas

Hamas is a Palestinian Islamic organization. It was created on the principles of Islamism, and they believed that Islam could gain momentum throughout the Arab world. Hamas was founded sometime in 1988.

The military wing of Hamas has launched attacks against Israeli soldiers and civilians. Tactics include suicide bombings, and since 2001, rocket attacks. Hamas's rocket arsenal has evolved from short-range, homemade Qassam rockets, to long-range weapons that have reached Israeli cities including Tel Aviv and Haifa.

In 2006, Hamas used an underground cross-border tunnel to capture an Israeli soldier, Gilad Shalit. They held him captive until 2011 when he was released in exchange for 1,027 Palestinian prisoners. Since then, Hamas has continued building a network of internal and cross-border tunnels, which are used to store and deploy weapons, shield militants, and facilitate cross-border attacks.

September the 11th attacks (9/11):

Background:

On September the 11th, 2001, there occurred the most significant terrorist attack of modern times from an American perspective, which had immediate and long-term significance and effects that can still be felt today.

Events:

On the morning of September the 11th, members of the Islamic terrorist organisation called Al-Qaeda hijacked four passenger planes. Two of the aeroplanes were crashed into the World Trade Centre in New York. The third plane was flown into a US military base called The Pentagon in Washington, D.C. We are still not sure of the location that had been targeted by the fourth plane, but it was believed to have been a building in Washington, D.C. This was due to the passengers overpowering the hijackers, and the plane crashing into a field. No one survived from any of the flights.

This had important consequences:

- The USA declared war on all terrorism.
- This declaration of war would lead to the invasion of Afghanistan and overthrowing the Taliban Government, which had hidden Al-Qaeda terrorists.
- This was then followed by the Second Gulf War, which was the invasion of Iraq and overthrowing the government led by Saddam Hussein who was allegedly supporting terrorism, especially Al-Qaeda.

High-Tech warfare:

The First Gulf War experienced the use of high-tech warfare. There were smart bombs, which were guided by laser beams. The only problem was that in smoke or dust, a big issue in the desert, it could refract or dissipate the laser, causing the weapon to veer off. The air campaign for Desert Storm lasted one month, and only 9% of the bombs dropped were smart bombs.

However, the First Gulf War was still decided with conventional weapons and tactics. Towards the end of the Gulf War, B-52s flew into Iraq and carpet-bombed military positions in the field with old-fashioned dumb bombs. Even then, the war was not won until about half a million in ground troops pushed the Iraqi army back across the border.

Modern Day Warfare or High-Tech Warfare consists of computerized weapons such as night vision, lasers, hacking, electronic warfare and state of the art weapons including drones and unmanned vehicles. Drones, also known as unmanned aerial vehicles, can be armed with a variety of devices, including high-resolution cameras, infrared cameras, and missiles. They can be piloted by pilots outside of the vehicle. They are known as joystick pilots because they watch screens and control the drone from ground control stations.

Other examples include:

The Joint Direct Attack Munition, (JDAM) is different to a laser-guided bomb. A JDAM is controlled by a Global Positioning Satellite (GPS) and can, therefore, hit its target in any weather or through the smoke.

A Joint Standoff Weapon (JSOW) is a missile that can be fired from 30,000 feet, has a 40-mile range and can be controlled whilst in flight. This allows it to hit mobile targets.

The High-Powered Microwave (HPM) releases up to two billion watts of electric energy in the form of a microwave, as much as the Hoover Dam generates in 24 hours. The impact of those microwaves will fry anything electrical within a fifth of a mile.

Despite the use of such weapons in Iraq and Afghanistan, they have not substantially reduced the dependence on conventional weapons and ground troops to defeat a determined enemy, as was seen in the First and Second Gulf Wars.

New wars and high-tech warfare

Definition of 'new' wars – war, criminality, a breakdown of community, challenges to human rights:

Bosnia 1992 - 1995

Background:

After World War Two, Serbia, Bosnia and Croatia were merged into one large state known as Yugoslavia, which also incorporated a large Muslim population left over from the Ottoman Empire. As the communist dictatorship of Tito declined further, calls for Nationalism and independence gained a voice. After the fall the Communism in the early 1990s, and by 1992, Bosnians, Croats and Bosniaks were demanding a referendum, which was eventually held but not recognised by the Bosnians who were the largest ethnic group in Yugoslavia. This was to eventually cause a civil war, with some historians arguing that a murder at a wedding was the first casualty of the Bosnian war.

War Crimes

Croats, Bosnians and Muslims turned upon one another. However, according to statistics, the Bosnians committed 90% of the genocides that took place during this war, and Croats 10%.

Ethnic cleansing

This can cover intimidation, forced expulsion, or killing of unwanted ethnic groups. So, in this case, Muslims, Bosnians, Croats and Bosniaks attacked one another, with an attempt to remove groups from certain areas of old Yugoslavia. In total, 2.2 million people were displaced.

Religious locations can also be destroyed, including cemeteries and cultural and historical buildings.

Rape

An estimated 12,000 - 20,000 women were raped by Bosnian Serb forces.

Aftermath and International Court of Justice:

In 2007, the International Court of Justice determined that Serbia had failed to prevent genocides committed by Serbian forces, it also was unable to punish them.

The rape of women was considered a form of weapon in war.

As a result, trials were held, and so far, 161 people have been convicted of war crimes resulting from the Bosnian war.

The War on Terror – aims, methods and results. Madrid (2004) and London (2005). World security measures:

Background:

Europe's involvement in the recent wars taking place in Afghanistan and Iraq. This 'war on terror' is arguably the reason for the attacks in Madrid and London. Muslims had enough of these wars and decided to use terror tactics to either push these countries into a broader war or to get them to remove themselves from the various conflicts in the Middle East, while also punishing citizens whom they felt were entangled in the conflicts. There is also an argument that this was a religious war, with the overall aim of eventually converting Europe into an Islamic state.

Madrid train bombings 2004 "11-M."

Aims:

There is limited information on the objectives, as the terrorists had operated on their own, not as part of a larger group. They have been linked to Al-Qaeda. However, other links have been made to other Spanish terrorist groups, including ETA. ETA is a Spanish terrorist organisation that wishes for the Northern part of Spain to separate away from the rest of Spain, to create a separate country. The Al-Qaeda group wanted to encourage Spain to join the Iraq war, with the overall aim of getting the whole of Europe and therefore Western Europe and America into a conflict in the Middle East. This would hopefully help to create a total rebellion against Westerners in the Middle East, removing them and further establishing a dominant Muslim political sphere of influence in the Middle East.

Methods:

4 locations and ten bombs were used. They were detonated using mobile phones, which set the explosives off at 7:37/38 in different trains across Madrid, during the morning rush hour, to create the maximum amount of damage.

Results:

193 people were killed, 143 of whom were Spanish. 1,800 were injured. Spain's pro-Iraq war government was removed from Office three days later. This was the last major terrorist attack by ETA to date.

London 2005 '7/7'

Aims:

One of the terrorists, Mohammad Sidique Khan, described his motivation. In a videotape, broadcast in September 2005, by Al Jazeera, the terrorists stated:

"I and thousands like me are forsaking everything for what we believe. Our drive and motivation don't come from tangible commodities that this world has to offer. Our religion is Islam, obedience to the one true God and following the footsteps of the final prophet messenger. Your democratically-elected governments continuously perpetuate atrocities against my people all over the world. Moreover, your support of them makes you directly responsible, just as I am directly responsible for protecting and avenging my Muslim brothers and sisters. Until we feel security, you will be our targets, and until you stop the bombing, gassing, imprisonment and torture of my people, we will not stop this fight. We are at war, and I am a soldier. Now you too will taste the reality of this situation."

Methods:

Suicide attack; four locations across the London were hit. Three underground trains were blown up at 8:49 am, and another bomb was blown up an hour later, on a bus.

Results:

18 people were killed and over 700 injured. The UK was put on high alert for years to come. There was an electrical power outage both in the underground railways and parts of the city. Finally, it had a significant impact on changing security policy and society's view of terrorism in Europe.

The importance of 'surgical' air strikes in the 21st-century wars in the Middle East.

Definition:

A surgical air strike is a military attack on another specific military target.

Battles in the Middle East

The United States has launched numerous surgical strikes in both Afghanistan and Iraq in the First and Second Gulf War using cruise missiles, although surgical strikes go further back than this.

So, from the beginning of the book do you have any thoughts on…

Barack Obama and drone attacks in Afghanistan?

Donald Trump and recent bombing raids in Afghanistan?

First and Second Gulf war

Use of drones (UAVs) role in Afghanistan, Pakistan and Iraq.

In 1991, during the First Gulf War in Iraq during the battle of Kuwait, for the first time, soldiers surrendered to an unmanned aerial vehicle on the island of Faylaka.

The development of drone wars in Pakistan and unmanned land vehicles (UGV/ unmanned ground vehicle) in Iraq and Afghanistan.

Remote controlled vehicles have made some significant progress in recent decades, but they had existed since World War Two when the Nazis used remote-controlled tank busters, known as Goliaths, that could be driven under a tank and exploded.

In the modern era, the primary aim of using these vehicles is to stop troops being killed, and to use robots to do surveillance, bomb disposal and increasing attacking enemy targets, especially in difficult to access locations and in urban areas.

Iraq and Afghanistan

When the invasion of Iraq in 2003 started, there were no UGVs. From 2004 to 2005 the number of UGV rose from 150 to 5,000. By 2008 there were 12,000. The army never considered these as capable of replacing soldiers during this period but did recognise that they would be instrumental in supporting troops, especially in both Iraq and Afghanistan. Both countries posed huge problems with the enemy not being in uniform and the areas of fighting being in mountainous regions and the urban regions. In 2004, in Fallujah, Iraq, it took 6 hours for one platoon of US troops to clear 54 houses. Considering there are 39,000 buildings in the city, a task like this is vast and challenging. More recently, the machines have been equipped with weapons to defend themselves or to neutralise threats. The other significant advantage, other than saving human life, is that they can cost just 10% of the cost of a human soldier. No food is required, no fear, they follow orders, can operate 24/7 and do not suffer from Post-Traumatic Stress Disorder. Finally, during operations in Iraq, they disarmed over 1000 roadside bombs. This was like the operations taking place in Afghanistan, which also required their use in destroying Improvised Explosive Devices. Improvised Explosive Devices were the weapon of choice in Afghanistan, which caused significant problems until the use of UGVs.

However, there is still no robot that can climb upstairs as quickly as a human, thus making clearing houses a complicated procedure. Optics can be heavily restricted; the comparison has been made of trying to drive a car using only a pair of binoculars. The machines require a second crew to be efficient, training on the machines is still in its infancy, and the issues of Artificial Intelligence are always something to think about and seriously to be considered. If they are to be used, there are significant potential difficulties. Who is responsible if the machine starts attacking the wrong targets or becomes self-aware?

Development of chemical, radiological and biological weapons:

Weapons of mass destruction

Weapons of mass destruction are weapons that could cause mass deaths and should not cause structural damage.

Chemical:

Agent Orange

The Agent Orange did clear the jungle, thus allowing the Americans to see the enemy more efficiently, but it also had the effect of destroying many innocent farmers' crops and killing their animals. The US used chemical weapons such as napalm (jellied petrol) and Agent Orange (superior strength weed killer) to clear jungles as this was the hiding place for the Vietcong. They also wanted to clear it from the Ho Chi Minh Trail, the route that the Vietcong used to get supplies from North Vietnam.

Napalm

The napalm did clear much of the undergrowth, but it also stuck to humans and caused horrific injuries.

Persian Gulf Syndrome also is known as Gulf War Syndrome

It consists of medical symptoms, supposedly related to fighting in and during the Gulf War. As reported, veterans have manifested the syndrome after they returned from their duty. The condition is often a controversial topic as some would not agree that such a syndrome genuinely exists. It is a rare kind of syndrome that doesn't happen to everyone.

Nerve Gas

Nerve gases are chemicals that are organic, which disrupt the nervous system in your body. The nerves in your body transfer messages to organs.

The nerve agent causes eyes to shut down, drooling, vomiting, involuntary urination and defecation. The first symptoms appear in seconds after exposure. Death by asphyxiation or cardiac arrest may follow in minutes due to the loss of the body's control over respiratory and other muscles. Some nerve agents are readily vaporised or aerosolised. Other than breathing, nerve agents can be absorbed through the skin.

Nerve agents are generally colourless to amber-coloured, tasteless liquids that may evaporate to a gas.

Radiological

A radiological weapon is any device that is designed to spread radioactive material with the intent to kill or cause destruction or both. According to the U.S. Department of Defence, an RDD is:

"any device, including any weapon or equipment, other than a nuclear explosive device, specifically designed to employ radioactive material by disseminating it to cause destruction, damage, or injury by means of the radiation produced by the decay of such material".

One type of RDD is an explosive combined with some radiological material, also known as a dirty bomb. It is not an actual nuclear weapon and does not yield the same explosive power. It uses conventional explosives to spread radioactive material, most commonly the spent fuels from nuclear power plants or radioactive medical waste.

It is, therefore, a weapon of mass disruption and potentially mass destruction. However, the range of damage is rather limited. If exploded, most deaths would come from the initial explosion, although that depends on the type of radiological material used.

Biological weapons are also known as germ weapons:

This is a weapon that could contain bacteria, viruses, toxins or even fungi. This form of warfare has existed for centuries, and although armies did not fully understand why arrows dipped in mud or bodies being thrown into castles and sieges caused disease, the effects were understood.

During World War One, Germany used some unusual tactics to infect cattle and horses coming from the United States and Allied armies on the Eastern and Western front.

This and the use of chemical weapons caused most countries to sign to the Geneva Protocol in 1925. This aimed at banning biological and chemical weapons.

In 1972, 170 states signed a treaty prohibiting the use of biological weapons.

Anthrax was a weaponised program that was an available weapon to the United States and the Soviet Union. During the First Gulf War, it was claimed that Saddam Hussein, the leader of Iraq, had developed anthrax weapons and other biological weapons agents such as smallpox.

Bibliography

https://qualifications.pearson.com/content/dam/pdf/International%20GCSE/History/2017/teaching-and-learning-materials/IGCSEHistory_Warfare_TopicBooklet.pdf

https://www.youtube.com/watch?v=1e_AZ3j2LbY HYPERLINK "https://www.youtube.com/watch?v=1e_AZ3j2LbY&index=39&list=PLYunlojkQXL7a1H0XivncLC4bw0VvEpUC"& HYPERLINK "https://www.youtube.com/watch?v=1e_AZ3j2LbY&index=39&list=PLYunlojkQXL7a1H0XivncLC4bw0VvEpUC"index=39 HYPERLINK "https://www.youtube.com/watch?v=1e_AZ3j2LbY&index=39&list=PLYunlojkQXL7a1H0XivncLC4bw0VvEpUC"& HYPERLINK "https://www.youtube.com/watch?v=1e_AZ3j2LbY&index=39&list=PLYunlojkQXL7a1H0XivncLC4bw0VvEpUC"list=PLYunlojkQXL7a1H0XivncLC4bw0VvEpUC

Tank Warfare on Iwo Jima by David E. Harper and Closing in: Marines in the seizure of Iwo Jima by Colonel Joseph H. Alexander.

http://trace.tennessee.edu/cgi/viewcontent.cgi?article=2252 HYPERLINK "http://trace.tennessee.edu/cgi/viewcontent.cgi?article=2252&context=utk_chanhonoproj"& HYPERLINK "http://trace.tennessee.edu/cgi/viewcontent.cgi?article=2252&context=utk_chanhonoproj"context=utk_chanhonoproj

Except as provided by the Copyright Act 1956, The Copyright, Designs and Patents Act 1988, Copyright and Related Rights Regulations 2003. No part of this publication may be reproduced, stored in a retrieval system or transmitted in any form or by any means without the prior written permission of the publisher.

Printed in Great Britain
by Amazon